Rain Forests
of the
World

Volume 7
Mangrove Forest–Orangutan

MARSHALL CAVENDISH
NEW YORK • LONDON • TORONTO • SYDNEY

Marshall Cavendish Corporation
99 White Plains Road
Tarrytown, New York
10591-9001

Website: www.marshallcavendish.com

Consulting Editors: Rolf E. Johnson, Nathan E. Kraucunas

Contributing Authors: Theresa Greenaway, Jill Bailey, Michael Chinery, Malcolm Penny, Mike Linley, Philip Steele, Chris Oxlade, Ken Preston-Mafham, Rod Preston-Mafham, Clare Oliver, Don Birchfield

Discovery Books
    Managing Editor: Paul Humphrey
    Project Editor: Gianna Williams
    Text Editor: Valerie Weber
    Designer: Ian Winton
    Cartographer: Stefan Chabluk
    Illustrators: Jim Channell, Stuart Lafford, Christian Webb

Marshall Cavendish
    Editor: Marian Armstrong
    Editorial Director: Paul Bernabeo

(cover) Salvin's Amazon Parrot

Editor's Note: Many systems of dating have been used by different cultures throughout history. *Rain Forests of the World* uses B.C.E. (Before Common Era) and C.E. (Common Era) instead of B.C. (Before Christ) and A.D. (Anno Domini, "In the Year of Our Lord") out of respect for the diversity of the world's peoples.

The publishers would like to thank the following for their permission to reproduce photographs:
362 Ronald Toms/Oxford Scientific Films, 363 William Gray/OSF, 364 P. K. Sharpe/OSF, 365 Michael Fogden/OSF, 366 Rod Williams/Bruce Coleman, 367 Bruce Coleman., 368 Frank Huber/OSF, 369 Jean-Leo Dugast/Panos Pictures, 370 Jerry Callow/Panos Pictures, 371 Nick Robinson/Panos Pictures, 372 Andrew Davies/Bruce Coleman, 373 & 374 Aldo Brando/OSF, 375 E. & D. Hosking/Frank Lane Picture Agency, 376 Daniel Heuclin/Natural History Photographic Agency, 377 M. P. L. Fogden/Bruce Coleman, 378 D. Ellinger/Foto Natura/FLPA, 379 & 380 Jany Sauvanet/NHPA, 381 M. Wendler/OSF, 382 & 383 Corbis Images, 384 Konrad Wothe/OSF, 385 Terry Whittaker/FLPA, 386 Alain Compost/Bruce Coleman, 387 Norbert Rosing/OSF, 388 Jean-Louis Le Moigne/NHPA, 389 & 390 Ken Preston-Mafham/Premaphotos Wildlife, 391 G. I. Bernard/NHPA, 392 John Shaw/NHPA, 393 Michael Fogden/OSF, 394 Mark Deeble and Victoria Stone/OSF, 395 Terry Whittaker/FLPA, 396 David Haring/OSF, 397 Morten Strange/NHPA, 398 & 399 Fred Hoogervorst/Panos Pictures, 400 Clive Shirley/Panos Pictures, 401 Ken Preston-Mafham/Premaphotos Wildlife, 402 Mary Evans Picture Library, 403 E. & D. Hosking/FLPA,404 Marie Read/Bruce Coleman, 405 Phil Ward/FLPA, 406 John Shaw/NHPA, 407 Andrew Devare/OSF, 408 Discovery Picture Library, 409 Len Robinson/FLPA, 410 Mantis Wildlife Films/OSF, 411 Discovery Picture Library, 412 Stephen Dalton/NHPA, 413 David Hosking/FLPA, 416 Morten Strange/NHPA, 417 P. Perry/FLPA, 418 Stan Osolinski/OSF, 419 Discovery Picture Library

Library of Congress Cataloging-in-Publication Data
Rain forests of the world.
        v.   cm.
        Includes bibliographical references and index.
        Contents: v. 1. Africa-bioluminescence—v. 2. Biomass-clear-cutting — v. 3. Climate and weather-emergent — v. 4. Endangered species-food web — v. 5. Forest fire-iguana — v.6. Indonesia-manatee — v. 7. Mangrove forest-orangutan — v. 8. Orchid-red panda — v. 9. Reforestation-spider — v. 10. Squirrel-Yanomami people — v. 11. Index.
                ISBN 0-7614-7254-1 (set)
                1. Rain forests—Encyclopedias. 1. Marshall Cavendish Corporation.
        QH86 .R39 2002
        578.734—dc21

    ISBN 0-7614-7254-1 (set)
    ISBN 0-7614-7261-4 (vol. 7)

Printed and bound in Italy

07 06 05 04 03 02   6 5 4 3 2 1

Contents

Mangrove Forest   362

Mantis   364

Marmoset and Tamarin   366

Maya People   368

Mbuti People   370

Medicinal Plant   372

Migration   376

Millipede   377

Mining   378

Miskito People   382

Mongoose   384

Monkey   385

Monsoon Rain Forest   389

Mosquito   391

Moss   392

Mudskipper   394

National Park   395

Natural Selection   401

Nest and Nest Building   403

New Zealand   406

Nocturnal Animal   407

North America   411

Nutrient Cycle   414

Oil Exploration   416

Okapi   418

Orangutan   419

Glossary   420

Index   421

Mangrove forests are found around tropical coasts and estuaries all over the world. They grow where the land meets the sea, gradually spreading seaward as their roots trap enough mud for new seedlings to grow. Other trees, such as the nipa palm, sundri, gewa, and goran trees of Southeast Asia, also grow in mangrove swamps. These forests provide critical barriers to tidal surges and storms, including hurricanes. They take the full force of the sea and wind, protecting the land behind them.

KEY FACTS

● **Mangroves grow best where the temperature does not fall below 68°F (20°C).**

● **Some mangrove seeds germinate while they are still on the tree. The torpedo-shaped seedlings plunge into the mud like spears, anchoring themselves firmly so that the tide cannot wash them away.**

● **The largest mangrove forest in the world is the Sundarbans in India and Bangladesh. Home to the Bengal tiger, the forest covers over 1,500 sq. mi. (4,000 km²).**

There are about 68 different species of mangroves. Like many rain forest plants, most mangroves have shiny, pointed leaves; a dense tangle of roots and low-growing branches trap mud and thus build up the coast.

Roots That Breathe

Tides regularly flood the seaward end of a mangrove forest, while the landward end lies in fresher water brought down by rivers. The retreating tide may expose extensive mudflats. Most of the nutrients lie in the surface layers of mud recently deposited by the tides, so shallow roots spread wide across the mud to gather the nutrients and anchor the tree.

Roots need oxygen, and oxygen is in short supply underwater. Many species of mangroves produce special breathing roots. Some produce prop roots that grow down from the stem near the mud, forming arching stilts. Little pores in the bark, called lenticels, absorb oxygen and transport it to the roots.

A mangrove swamp in the Seychelles. The mangrove roots trap mud, which builds up so that other species less tolerant of flooding can move in.

Other species of mangroves, such as *Sonneratia*, have "knees"—knobbly, kneelike roots that rise up from the mud into the air and back down again.

Mangroves must also cope with salty water. They need to expel salt, just like people do. If salt levels are too high, animal and plant tissues dry out (dehydrate). Some mangroves filter out the salt using their roots, while others store it in leaves that are occasionally shed. A few have special salt glands that expel the salt onto the leaf surface, where it gets washed away by the tides.

Daily Migrations

The shallow, sheltered waters of the mangrove swamps are rich in nutrients—organic matter in the form of dead leaves and flowers shed by the mangroves, and minerals washed in with the mud. These swampy forests do not support the great variety of animal species found in other tropical forests, but the maze of roots and stems provides shelter for some forest animals as well as for seashore creatures such as oysters and mussels, which anchor themselves to the prop roots and knees.

Many of the mangrove forest's inhabitants have adapted to the rising and falling of the tide. In mangrove swamps from Africa to India, mudskippers skitter across the mud in search of crabs and worms. When the tide comes in, bringing with it large predatory fish, mudskippers may climb mangrove roots to escape. At this time, small fish, shrimp, prawns, and jellyfish replace them in the water.

Bigger animals live in mangrove swamps, too. Deer, such as the Asian chital (CHEE-duhl), feed there, as do the tigers, leopards, and other cats that hunt them. Fruit bats roost in mangroves, and

so do thousands of birds, which feed on the worms, shellfish, and fish of the mudflats. The Caroni swamp of Trinidad, for example, is home to 10,000 scarlet ibis. Frigate birds, boobies, egrets, and cormorants all flourish in these forests.

Coasts Under Threat

Large areas of mangroves are being cut down to make room for fish and prawn farms. Other areas are being cleared for growing rice. Mangrove trees provide wood for charcoal, making paper, house posts, scaffold poles for the Japanese construction industry, firewood, and bark for tanning leather. With the loss of the mangroves, coastal waters become muddier and coral reefs begin to die from the lack of sunlight. Storms and tidal surges penetrate farther inland, flooding valuable farmland with salt water.

Check these out:
Crustacean   Mudskipper   Root

Mantis

Mantises are predatory insects. They are sometimes called praying mantises because when lying in wait for their prey, they often hold their forelimbs in front of their face as if they are praying. The largest mantises include species of *Archimantis* that may exceed 6 inches (15 cm) in length. At the other end of the scale are tiny mantises no more than half an inch (1 cm) long that pick aphids (AE-fuhds) from the underside of leaves.

The shielding flap covering the thorax of this mantis from Costa Rica makes it look extremely leaflike from above—a useful camouflage.

Although a few mantises chase their prey, the majority sit still and wait for a victim to come within range. The mantis watches its prey carefully, continually turning its head and flexible neck to look directly at the approaching insect. When the victim is close enough, the mantis's spiky front legs shoot out and back in a flash, snapping shut around the prey and trapping it firmly between the spikes. The mantis's powerful jaws then cut the victim into small pieces, munching easily through hard legs and even the tough wing cases of beetles. Although their eyes can pick up the slightest movement, they are not good at detecting shapes; a mantis will often walk right past a resting insect as long as the prey keeps still.

Camouflage for Attack and Defense
Mantises are experts at camouflage, which helps them hide from their prey as well as from their enemies. Bark mantises are brown and flat, blending in with the tree trunks they live on. Several other brown species have crinkled wings and ragged growths on their neck and

364

This colorful slender flower mantis from Malaysia can easily be mistaken for a withered leaf or petal. The spines on its front legs are clearly visible.

look remarkably like dead leaves clinging to branches. Most mantises, however, are some shade of green. They wait for prey among the leaves, although they often position themselves close to flowers where they are more likely to find prey.

Some mantises are more colorful, with pink and cream mixing with or replacing the green. These insects, which include the airplane or target mantises of Africa and Asia, sit in bunches of flowers to wait for their prey. Some of their nymphs can even change color to match different flowers. The pink or white orchid mantis of Southeast Asia takes its camouflage even further. Broad flaps on its legs resemble petals; the whole mantis can easily be mistaken for a flower. Other insects are attracted to it wherever it sits, so it rarely goes hungry.

Dangerous Mating

Male mantises are usually smaller than females, and they are sometimes eaten by their partners even before they have finished mating, although not

all mantis species partake in such cannibalism. After mating, the female lays her eggs in a mass of froth that gradually hardens into a tough protective case. The baby mantises that emerge look like ants, and at first they feed on aphids and other small insects.

IN FOCUS

Hissing Defense

If camouflage fails, many mantises have a second line of defense. They lift their wings and rub their abdomen up and down against them to produce a loud hissing sound, which is enough to frighten most small birds. At the same time, the mantis might display scary eyespots on its front wings.

Check these out:

- Camouflage
- Courtship
- Insect
- Insectivore
- Invertebrate

Marmosets (MAHR-muh-sets) and tamarins (TA-muh-ruhns) are members of a family of squirrel-like South American monkeys that live primarily in the rain forest of the upper Amazon River basin; only three species live outside Amazonia, in Colombia and Central America. Marmosets and tamarins have long sharp claws rather than short flat toenails on all except their big toes, an adaptation for climbing large trees. Marmosets have large incisors, equal in size to their canines, while tamarins' canine teeth are longer. Both have long silky fur, and both feed on fruits, insects, and occasionally small mammals.

KEY FACTS

● The destruction of their rain forest home for agriculture and housing threatens all marmosets and tamarins.

● The smallest marmoset, the pygmy marmoset, is about 11 in. (28 cm) long from head to tail and weighs just over 6 oz. (190 g).

● The golden lion tamarin is the emblem of conservation in Brazil.

Marmosets

The most numerous animals in the group are the common marmosets. Their black-and-white bodies are between 3 and 12 inches (8 and 30 cm) long, and their tails extend nearly twice that length. Weighing about 2¼ pounds (1 kg), they have round heads with flat faces and thick, white tufts on their ears.

Other marmosets' coats vary in color from white to black or reddish, often with rings on their tails. The smallest is the pygmy marmoset, which is 11 inches (28 cm) long from head to tail and weighs just over 6 ounces (190 g).

Both tamarins and marmosets spend as much as a third of their feeding time hunting in clumps of leaves and holes in trees for animals such as frogs, lizards, spiders, and insects. Marmosets also follow army ants, catching insects disturbed by the ant swarms. Pygmy marmosets have a more specialized diet: they spend much of their time digging holes in trees to eat the sap and gum that oozes out.

The pygmy marmoset is the smallest living monkey. It lives in forests that are liable to flood and along riverbanks.

An emperor tamarin shows off its magnificent mustache.

Tamarins

Tamarins are larger than marmosets, between 8 and 14 inches (20 and 35 cm) long, with a tail up to almost 16 inches (40 cm) long. They are also much more striking in appearance: the emperor tamarin has long gray fur, with a reddish tail and a magnificent white mustache. The best-known is the golden lion tamarin, named after its thick mane and golden, silky fur. One reason it is so well known is that it is very rare.

Only about 400 golden lion tamarins remain in the wild, in one small area of Brazilian rain forest northeast of Rio de Janeiro. Most of their habitat has been destroyed for plantations, cattle ranching, and housing. The patches of forest left are too small to support populations of tamarins large enough to prevent inbreeding. Inbreeding can reduce the long-term fitness of the species, since breeding pairs are too closely related and resulting offspring are prone to genetic defects.

Breeding Programs

In the past tamarins were captured to be sold as pets, although they are difficult to keep healthy in captivity. However, many zoos in the world have discovered how to keep them fit and even to breed them. This has been the key to the possible survival of this rare and beautiful little animal. In 1991 the Golden Lion Tamarin Species Survival Plan was set up to breed the species in captivity, and 140 organizations all over the world are taking part. Since the plan started, the original 70 captive tamarins have multiplied to 500.

To improve the tamarins' chances, landowners are encouraged to create strips of forest between their plantations to provide corridors so that separate populations can meet and interbreed. The golden lion tamarin is now the emblem of conservation in Brazil.

IN FOCUS

Dining Companions

Two species of tamarins, the emperor and the saddle-back, almost always feed together in the forests of southeastern Peru. Since they eat the same food, they would be expected to compete. However, scientists think that eating together helps both species because it avoids one troop wasting energy by going to feed on a tree that the other has just stripped of fruit.

Check these out:
- Amazonia ● Endangered Species
- Mammal ● Monkey ● Primate

The Maya (MIE-ah) are a native people of the tropical rain forest of a large portion of northern Central America and parts of Mexico. They have inhabited this land since sometime before 1000 B.C.E. Slash-and-burn agriculture in the rain forest allowed the Maya to build one of the world's great ancient civilizations, which peaked about 700 C.E. At that time the Maya population numbered about one million people.

The ancient Maya built large stone pyramids and temples, creating pockets of civilization within the rain forest. They made impressive achievements in mathematics and astronomy, created a very accurate calendar, and used a written language with pictographs. They also developed advanced agricultural methods, growing corn, beans, and squash. Cotton crops provided material for their clothing. Eventually the Maya abandoned their cities when they were not able to grow

KEY FACTS

● **Many centuries ago the Maya built a great civilization in the rain forests of Central America.**

● **In Guatemala each Maya village has its own distinctive style of dress.**

● **There are only 500 Lacandon Maya people still living in southern Mexico.**

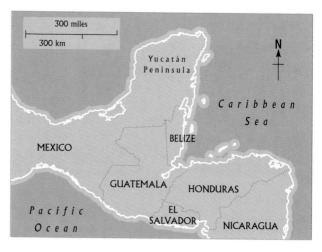

Maya women fetch water from a community well in Yucatán, Mexico.

IN FOCUS

The God House

In Lacandon Maya culture, the god house is the center of ceremonial life. Built in a clearing near the village, the structure has open sides and a thatched roof. In addition to housing ceremonies, it is also where ceremonial objects are stored. One ceremony involves drinking the sacramental beverage called *balche* (BAL-chae) and praying to the gods. The beverage is brewed in a container called a *chem* (KIM), built on the east side of the god house.

enough food to feed the population, and the rain forest reclaimed them.

The Maya people still live throughout a large part of Central America in Guatemala, Belize, El Salvador, and Honduras, and in southern Mexico and the Yucatán Peninsula. Among the approximately 22 different languages spoken by Maya peoples are 4 main languages—Quiche, Mam, Tzutujil, and Cakchiquel.

In Guatemala each Maya village has its own style of dress. The women make clothing featuring the distinctive designs of their village.

The True People

In southern Mexico the Lacandon Maya, who call themselves *Hach Winik* ("True People"), still maintain a close connection to the rain forest, despite being resettled by the government. Their numbers have been reduced to about 500 people living in three main villages.

One of these villages, Lacanjá Chansayab, stands at the edge of the largest remaining tract of rain forest in the region, which is called the Monte Azules Biosphere Reserve. The Lacandons are the only people who are allowed to hunt in the reserve. In addition to harvesting its animal and plant resources for food, they also use the reserve for its medicinal plants.

Another Lacandon village, Najá, which is located near Lake Najá, maintains traditional Maya customs, including the practice of polygamy. Ceremonies are held in a building called a god house. While in the god house, Lacandons speak in a special prayer voice that has melody and music in its tones.

A Maya girl displays the colorful clothing of her Guatemalan village.

Check these out:

● **Central America** ● **People of the Rain Forest** ● **Resettlement**

Mbuti People

The Ituri and Lindi Rivers rise in eastern Democratic Republic of the Congo in central Africa. They flow westward before joining the mighty Congo River on its journey to the sea. The lands that drain into them are densely forested and lie just north of the equator. About 27,000 square miles (70,000 km²) of these forests are home to a people called the Mbuti (em-BOO-tee). Expert at forest survival, the Mbuti tend to be small-featured, lightweight, and short. Adults tend to be between about 54 and 62 inches (138 and 158 cm) tall.

KEY FACTS

● **The Mbuti may have the oldest history of any ethnic group now living in Africa.**

● **After centuries of dealing with the Bantu-speaking villagers who live on the edges of the forest, the Mbuti now speak Bantu instead of their own language.**

● **Among the foods gathered by the Mbuti are termites and soft-bodied insects, which are rich in protein.**

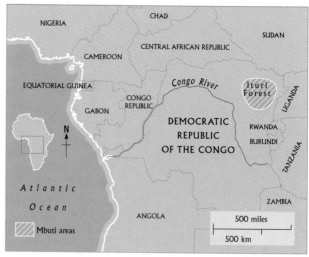

To the Mbuti the rain forest has always been a safe haven that has provided for all their needs. Today this is still mostly true, but for at least part of the year, the Mbuti visit Bantu villages to exchange forest produce for farmed crops such as plantains and other supplies.

Deep in the Forest

The Mbuti spend most of the year in the forest in bands of up to 40 people. All members of the hunting band work together; there are no chiefs. The men

A Mbuti hunter waits with bow and arrows in the forest near Komanda, in the Ituri River region of the eastern Democratic Republic of the Congo.

Mbuti hunters pause to prepare an antelope carcass that they have killed.

Threats to the Future

The forest that has sustained the Mbuti for thousands of years is now under threat. As the population of the farming villages grows, the Mbuti are expected to provide them with more and more food from the forest, and overhunting has reduced wildlife numbers. Newcomers now enter the forest—mining prospectors, loggers in search of quality hardwood, cotton and coffee planters, and soldiers during times of political strife and war. The new arrivals bring diseases to which the Mbuti have little immunity. They disturb both plants and animals—loggers and miners strip the land, while soldiers may kill animals for food—and threaten the villagers' way of life.

IN FOCUS

Crafts, Song, and Dance

The Mbuti are great storytellers and love to dance. Either alone or together, they sing about hunting and the forest wildlife they know so well. Song and dance also accompany long religious rituals called *molimo* used during a time of crisis or death. Other ceremonies give thanks to the forest, or honor ancestors. They blow a sacred trumpet made from a tube of wood to mark their rituals.

smoke out wild bees so they can collect the honeycombs. They hunt with bows and arrows and trap wild animals with snares and nets, killing forest antelopes, monkeys, and porcupines. As the chief gatherers and cooks, women search for forest fruits, roots, mushrooms, and herbs. They act as beaters, too, driving game into the hunters' nets. Women also build the Mbuti's small, dome-shaped shelters of saplings covered in leaves.

Check these out:

● Africa ● Congo ● Disease ● Homes in the Rain Forest ● Hunter-Gatherer
● People of the Rain Forest

371

Medicinal Plant

Both archaeological and written historical evidence shows that humans have used plants for medicinal purposes for many thousands of years. The first such plants were probably discovered by accident, when someone tried a plant to see if it was edible only to discover that it cured some ill from which they were suffering.

Why are tropical forests an important source of medicinal plants? One reason is that such forests contain a high percentage of the total number of plant species living today. The more species, the greater the chance that some of them might produce chemicals useful for medicines. In addition, many insects and other animals eat rain forest plants. To defend themselves from these animals, some plants have evolved potent chemicals that give them an unpleasant taste or are even poisonous. Some of these defensive chemicals have proved to be important as medicines.

KEY FACTS

● The remains of medicinal plants have been found in archaeological sites that are at least 8,000 years old.

● About four-fifths of the world's population today still rely on native plants for their supplies of medicine.

● So far, scientists have analyzed about one percent of rain forest plant species to see if they contain useful medicinal compounds.

An area of rain forest in Belize being tested by western pharmaceutical companies. These companies are searching for plants that may have medicinal uses.

pouring boiling water over leaves, bark, or some other part of a particular plant. If the medicine contains substances that would quickly evaporate, the infusion is drunk immediately. If not, it is left for a while, much like teas, until all the active ingredients have dissolved into the water.

Many natural chemicals will not dissolve in water, but they will dissolve in alcohol. Using another method, the forest peoples therefore produce medicines called *garrafadas*. They grind up a particular plant or several plants and allow them to soak for several days in one of the native alcoholic beverages until the active chemicals have dissolved out.

Early Discoveries

One of the first, and most important, medicinal plants to come out of the rain forest was quinine. After Spain had conquered much of South America, the Spanish sent shiploads of bark from trees in the high rain forests of the Andes to Europe. The bark came from cinchona (sing-KOE-nuh) trees and was referred to as Indian fever bark. When soaked in water, the bark produced a medicine that was used to treat all kinds of fever, especially malaria. People later discovered that the bark contained quinine, the cure for malaria. So much bark was taken from South America that the cinchona trees were nearly wiped out. Luckily they grow just as well in other warm parts of the world, such as India and Southeast Asia. There, trees grown in large plantations supply the world's demand for the bark.

Traditional Medicines

Amazonian peoples prepare their medicines in several ways. One common method is to produce an infusion by

IN FOCUS

Word of Mouth

Unlike Westerners, the native peoples of the world's rain forests cannot call a doctor when illness strikes. Instead they rely upon their knowledge of the healing properties of the plants that grow in the forest around them. Since nothing is written down, which plants are which, where they grow in the forest, when they should be collected, and how they are used has to be passed on by word of mouth from parents to their children.

Today the medicine may be bottled and sold to other members of the community.

Native Amazonians also produce healing syrups by cooking medicinal plants with a little sugar and water. As with Western syrupy medicines, they are often used to treat coughs, colds, and other chest problems. Sometimes these peoples extract juices from leaves or other parts of plants and use them immediately, probably because the juices lose their medicinal effect if they are left to stand. Amazonians also use fresh, sticky latexes that leak out of some plants when they are cut. These latexes, known to local people as *amapa* and *sucuuba*, act as tonics to strengthen the lungs and as anti-inflammatories.

A native South American prepares medicine from vines and leaves. He mashes them and then boils them in water for about twelve hours.

In recent years aromatherapy has become popular in the West. People add fragrant oils to bathwater, perfumes, or candles; the scents released can make them feel better emotionally as well as physically. Aromatherapy is traditional among some of the Amazon peoples.

Research has shown that while some of these native therapies help to cure some ailments, many of them simply make the patient feel better emotionally, which can in turn lead to physical improvements. It is the traditional forest medicines that have a direct physical effect that interest most Western pharmaceutical companies.

Modern Medicines

A number of important drugs have been discovered in tropical rain forest plants. Some South American Indian peoples coat the tips of their arrows with the juice from

certain plants. The juice contains the poison curare (kyuh-RAHR-ee), which makes muscles relax. When a monkey is hit by an arrow, it is forced to let go of the branch on which it is sitting and falls to the ground. Doctors now use a synthetic form of curare in hospitals, given as an injection, to relax patients before a major operation. A different kind of drug is produced from a yam that grows wild in the forests of Mexico. Chemicals called phytoestrogens taken from these yams were used to make the first birth-control pills.

Expensive Research

Currently only about one percent of the plants growing in the world's rain forests have been tested to see if they contain chemicals that might make useful medicines. This could mean that out there somewhere in the other 99 percent, cures for many human ailments are waiting to be discovered.

Whether they ever will be depends upon a number of factors. First, of course, the rain forests are being cut down, disappearing at an alarming rate; it is almost a certainty that we have already lost forever plant species that may have yielded important drugs. Second, it is extremely expensive to find and develop a drug. Unless the wealthy countries of the

Rosy Periwinkle

The rosy periwinkle grows wild in the forests of Madagascar. This plant has been used for generations as a medicine by the local peoples but was largely ignored by people in the West. It was only in the 1960s that chemists analyzed the plant and found that it produced two chemicals, vinblastine and vinchristine, which are now important in controlling leukemia in children. Before the drug was developed, four out of five children died from leukemia. Today the drug cures the same number. The plant is now cultivated in India where native Madagascan pests cannot attack it.

world are prepared to invest in careful research, lifesaving medicines may not be discovered before most of the rain forest has been destroyed.

Check these out:

● Biotechnology ● Disease ● Madagascar

Migration

Migration is the movement of an animal population from one place to another at a regular time of year. Seasonal changes in the weather usually trigger migration. However, because there are no marked seasons in the rain forest, this type of migration does not happen there. Instead animals may move about in the forest to avoid—or to seek out—places that become flooded. Some parts of the upper Amazon rain forest, for example, flood at certain times of year. When this happens, fish move out of the rivers to lay their eggs among the tree trunks, where leaf-litter insects provide their young with plenty of food. Waterbirds, such as wood storks and wood ibises, move regularly between the Amazon and the Orinoco Rivers, preferring to be close to these rivers while their water level is lowest so that they have more mud to explore for food.

Finding Food

In Borneo's rain forest, a spell of dry weather in a particular place can trigger a fruiting season, when many different kinds of trees produce fruit at the same time. These sudden gluts of food happen at different times in different parts of the forest. Bearded pigs migrate in huge herds to feed on fallen fruit.

Birds that feed on nectar, such as hummingbirds in the American Tropics and sunbirds in Africa and Asia, may migrate to the rain forest during the peak flowering season of their favorite food plants, then move away to breed when the peak is past. Insect-eating birds, such as tyrant flycatchers and yellow-green vireos, visit the Amazon rain forest at the same time, when the abundance of nectar attracts plenty of insects. They nest some way to the north in Mexico and Costa Rica. Many species of small birds, such as warblers and flycatchers, live in temperate zones but migrate to the Tropics in wintertime.

Migrating People

People also migrate in the rain forest. The Guahibo (gwah-HEE-boe) and the Chiricoa (cheer-ee-KOE-ah) Indians live along the Orinoco River in eastern Colombia, where they move from cultivating crops to fishing to hunting as the seasons change. When the river is too high for fishing, they move to the savanna to plant crops. While the crops grow, they hunt in the forest.

Bearded pigs are migratory feeders: herds of them roam long distances in search of food.

Check these out:
● Flooding ● Pig and Peccary ● River ● Season

Millipede

The word *millipede* literally means "1,000 legs," but no millipede ever has that many. Even the 8-inch (20-cm) monsters that roam the rain forests rarely have more than about 250 legs, although the record is held by a South African species with 710 legs. A millipede's slender body is made up of numerous rings, or segments, and except for a few segments at the front and the rear, each one carries two pairs of legs. On a millipede's head are a pair of short, clubbed antennae.

Most millipedes are slow-moving scavengers, living mainly on the ground and feeding on decaying vegetation. They play a major role in the breakdown of dead leaves on the forest floor. Some climb trees at night to nibble algae and debris in bark crevices.

Although most millipedes are black or brown and rather dull, some have brightly colored bands that warn predators of their unpleasant flavor. Glands along the sides of the body secrete fluids with foul smells and tastes. Some species even emit cyanide and other deadly poisons that can kill other animals that venture too close. The secretions generally ooze from the millipedes' bodies, but some of the big tropical species can fire them out in a fine spray that can travel as far as 3 feet (1 m). The spray can burn an animal's skin, and it can cause blindness if it gets into the eyes. People in tropical Mexico grind up one species of millipede to use as an arrow poison.

Despite the poisons, toads and some birds eat millipedes. Lorises from the rain forests of Southeast Asia also eat them—but not before rubbing them roughly with their paws to get rid of most of the poison. Nonpoisonous millipedes may have other defenses. Pill millipedes can roll up into balls for protection; some tropical species roll up into a sphere as big as a golf ball.

The bright colors of this giant Brazilian millipede warn birds and other animals that its body is packed with poisons.

Check these out:
- Decomposer ● Forest Floor
- Invertebrate

Mining is the extraction of minerals from the rocks that make up the earth's surface. The minerals are mined for use as fuels (such as coal) or because they contain valuable metals, such as iron, aluminum, copper, tin, and gold, or precious stones, such as diamonds and emeralds. Mining operations include not only extracting minerals from the ground but also industrial processes such as smelting and transportation. Most of the major rain forests of the world are suffering from mining activities, particularly in South America and Africa.

KEY FACTS

● Processing and smelting plants, roads, and other mining needs use about 30 times the area of land that's actually required to extract the minerals.

● Important minerals found in rain forests include coal, iron, copper, aluminum, and gold.

● Indigenous peoples are moved from their land by miners, catch diseases from them, and are poisoned by chemicals used in mineral processing.

Although the soil in most rain forests is poor in minerals, the rocks underneath often contain amounts attractive to mining companies. The rocks of the Amazon River basin, for example, contain large quantities of iron and aluminum.

There are two main ways of extracting minerals. Strip-mining is used to extract mineral deposits close to the surface, and deep mining is used to extract mineral deposits deep underground. In strip-mining, explosives turn the rock to rubble, and enormous excavating machines dig out and carry away the rubble, exposing the mineral veins. In deep mining, miners working in

Small–scale gold mining, like this operation in French Guiana, destroys forest and churns up the soil.

tunnels use drills and cutting machines.

The last quarter of the 20th century saw a large expansion in mining activities in rain forest countries. Mining is portrayed as being important for the economic development of these countries. However, it is often the large, powerful, multinational companies that profit from mining. In fact, the companies that pay fees to mine the land are often paid to do that mining by the countries'

A huge area of Brazilian forest has been cleared to extract gold–bearing rocks. It will take hundreds of years for the forest to regrow.

governments; the money just circulates between the company and the government. Local people usually suffer, gaining no income and losing their traditional hunting and farming lands to the mines and their health to diseases carried by the miners.

Effects of Mining

Mining creates many problems in the rain forest itself. Loggers fell trees to allow space for mines, and mining machines and processes create pollution.

Ores that are dug from the ground are often mixtures of different minerals, so the ore must be processed to remove unwanted materials. Smelting is the process of removing a metal from its ore by melting. For example, iron ore is melted to extract the iron. Iron-smelting furnaces require large amounts of charcoal

IN FOCUS

Spreading Diseases

The effects of mining on indigenous rain forest people has been disastrous. Not only is their way of life disrupted, but mine workers also bring diseases, such as measles and influenza (flu), into the rain forest—diseases to which indigenous people have no resistance. The rapidly built shantytowns where the miners live, with their poor sanitation, are breeding grounds for other diseases.

for heat. In rain forest countries, millions of trees surrounding the smelting plant are felled and burned to make this charcoal. Extracting aluminum from its ore, bauxite, requires large amounts of electricity. Often, huge hydroelectric dams are built on rivers to provide electricity, and their reservoirs flood more areas of forest.

Roads, railroads, and airstrips are built to carry mining machinery, ore from mines to processing and smelting factories, and workers from towns to mines. These cover only narrow strips of land, but they are the starting points for more erosion of the fragile soil. Slash-and-burn farmers and cattle ranchers move in and clear the land next to the roads. Overall, processing and smelting plants, roads, and other mining needs use about 30 times the area of land needed for actually extracting the minerals.

Mining activities, especially strip-mining, cause deforestation, although far less than logging, slash-and-burn farming, or cattle ranching. Once the trees and fragile soil have been removed, there is little chance of the forest recovering when the miners have moved on. The mine workings also encourage soil erosion in the surrounding forest, since the trees with their soil-holding roots have been felled. Some mining companies try to reduce damage by removing the topsoil before strip-mining, replacing it carefully afterward and replanting the vegetation with seeds from a nearby preserved forest.

Amazonian Gold

Some areas of the Amazon River basin contain large gold deposits. The gold is not mined in an organized, large-scale way but by individual miners or small groups of miners called *garimpeiros*. Most garimpeiros are from Brazil's big cities, hoping to make their fortunes quickly. Few are successful. Tens of thousands of workers have moved onto land on the Brazil-Venezuela border, working and

Wood cut from the surrounding rain forest is burned slowly in these ovens, where it turns to charcoal. The charcoal is used for iron smelting.

new towns for miners, and railroads to transport iron to the coast have all sprung up. The worst effect on the rain forest is probably the cutting down of millions of trees to make charcoal for the smelters. About 900 square miles (2,300 km²) of trees are cut down every year to feed the iron-smelting plants used in this project. That is the size of a large capital city and its suburbs.

Processing machines like this one in Brazil wash tiny amounts of gold out of rock. The waste rock and water forms huge muddy pools.

living in squalid conditions. Using hydraulic mining to remove mineral deposits from the ground, they wash the sludge down chutes that allow gold to settle out and be collected. Using mercury, they purify the gold. These small-scale mining operations create huge problems in the rain forest. The stagnant pools left by the hydraulic mining allow mosquitoes to breed, increasing the risk of the disease malaria carried by these insects. The mercury, which is poisonous, leaks into the ground and is washed into rivers, where it enters the food chain, causing illnesses and death among both animals and humans.

The Grand Carajas Program

Under the rain forests of Par State in eastern Brazil is one of the world's largest deposits of iron ore; it also has deposits of aluminum and copper. The Grand Carajás Program is designed to extract, process, and smelt these ores. It began in the mid-1970s and is still continuing. Industrial plants, hydroelectric dams to provide electricity,

IN FOCUS

Rehabilitating Mines

Mineracao Rio do Norte bauxite mine in Brazil began operating in the 1970s. During the first nine years, the company discharged the bauxite tailings, ore residues that had been crushed and chemically treated to extract the ore, into a natural lake 19 mi. (30 km) away from the mine. Then in the 1980s, the company began a program of rehabilitation: seeds were collected and grown in a nursery and then transplanted to leveled, mined-out areas. Topsoil was either retained or replaced. Instead of washing out the tailings into the water supply, the company filled mined-out areas with the tailings. After nine years the tailings were sufficiently consolidated for planting vegetation above. The lake that had been contaminated over the years with bauxite tailings was rehabilitated with a mixture of fertilizer, seeds, and mycorrhizal fungi and bacteria.

Check these out:

● Disease ● Exploitation ● Human Interference ● Pollution ● Resettlement

Miskito People

The Miskito, (meess-KEE-toe), also called Mosquito, are a native people of the tropical rain forest of the Caribbean coast of Central America. They live along the eastern coast of Nicaragua and the northeastern coast of neighboring Honduras. This area is called the Miskito Coast.

A History of Turmoil

Before the Spanish invaded Nicaragua in 1522, the Miskito were one of many different Indian groups living in the highland valleys of western Nicaragua. The total population of Indians living in that area has been estimated at between half a million and 1.5 million people.

When the Spanish came, they divided the Indians among themselves into a kind of forced-labor system called the *encomienda* (en-koe-mee-EHN-duh). However, Miskitos refused to participate and moved far beyond the reach of the Spanish, to the other side of swamps and dense rain forest on the Caribbean coast.

In the Treaty of Managua in 1860, Nicaragua formally recognized the Miskito Coast as land reserved for the Miskito people. However, during the 1970s and 1980s, civil war in Nicaragua greatly disrupted the Miskitos' lives.

KEY FACTS

● Miskito houses are built on stilts, elevated off the ground by about 4 ft. (1.2 m).

● Nicaragua's government granted the Miskitos land of their own in 1860.

● Many young Miskito men court their partners by serenading them.

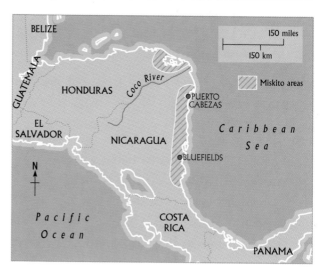

Miskito Daily Life

Most Miskitos live in small villages along the coast or on riverbanks. About a quarter of the people live in two seaports, Bluefields in the south and Puerto Cabezas in the north.

A Miskito village on the coast of the Caribbean Sea.

The Miskitos are mostly an agricultural people. Rice and beans are the major crops, but they also raise bananas, coffee, sugarcane, and pineapples. Hunting and fishing provide important proteins for their diet.

In the small, traditional Miskito villages, family life is very important. The husband is the recognized head of the household. The wife will not walk beside her husband but is always careful to walk at least one step behind him.

Most people in the village are related to one another. When a young man wants to find a young woman to court, he will go to a neighboring village. There, he will try to win a young woman's favor with presents. If that doesn't work, he will serenade her with songs.

Building a Home

Miskito houses have changed greatly during the last few centuries, but the rain forest still provides the Miskito with their primary building materials. Originally Miskitos relied more on hunting than on agriculture, so they were a more nomadic people. Thus their houses were simple shelters that could be built quickly, usually a lean-to with a roof thatched with palm leaves.

These sea turtles have been caught by Miskito fishermen.

Today the Miskitos have settled village sites with much more permanent housing. The roofs are still thatched with palm leaves, but they are much larger and made with sloping or peaked bamboo frames. The villagers also use bamboo to build the frame for the rest of the house. The house itself sits on stilts, elevated off the ground by about 4 feet (1.2 m).

It is not unusual for a Miskito house to actually be two different buildings, both elevated on stilts and connected to one another by ramps. One building is used for cooking, and the other is used for sleeping.

Check these out:
- Central America ● Homes in the Rain Forest ● People of the Rain Forest ● Resettlement

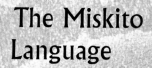

IN FOCUS

The Miskito Language

In keeping with their long history of separation from the rest of Nicaragua, Miskitos have resisted learning the Spanish language. They prefer that their schools give instruction in Miskito or in English. The Miskito language remains the dominant language in their land.

Mongoose

Mongooses are mammals that belong to the same family as genets and civets. They are native to Africa, Madagascar, and Asia and have been introduced to the West Indies. They generally inhabit dry, open thornbush country, though a number of species are found in rain and monsoon forests.

Mongooses have a long pointed snout, bright beady eyes, and small, rounded ears. Their slim, sinuous body has short legs and a long, often bushy, tail, giving them a slinky, low-slung appearance.

Although a few mongooses are nocturnal, most kinds are active during the day. Some species travel in large conspicuous groups, trotting through the forest, sniffing out signs of a meal. Most of their food is located on the ground, but if necessary, they will climb into low trees to raid birds' nests.

Hunting for Prey

Extremely efficient hunters, some mongooses will even bite and kill deadly scorpions. The Indian stripe-necked mongoose hunts chital (CHEE-duhl) fawns. Some kinds of mongooses slay snakes, including even the most poisonous and dangerous types, such as cobras. The lightning-quick movements of the mongoose, plus its habit of wearing the snake down and tiring it out, ensure its success in such a risky contest. Once the snake becomes too exhausted to strike, it lowers its head, and the mongoose makes its final pounce, biting the snake in the neck. Some mongooses drink the blood of their prey.

The rusty red ring-tailed mongoose is widespread in the forests of Madagascar but is not found anywhere else. Active in daytime, small family parties of two or three individuals are often seen, especially when they boldly turn up at forest camps for a food handout. Like many mongooses, they will eat just about anything of animal origin, including frogs, lizards, young birds, eggs, many kinds of insects, snakes, and fish, as well as fruit when it becomes available. The crab-eating mongoose from Assam in India and Nepal lives beside forested streams where it catches crabs, breaking open their tough shells by knocking them against rocks.

The striking rust–colored ring–tailed mongoose from Madagascar will sometimes climb trees in search of a meal.

Check these out:
- Carnivore
- Civet
- Mammal

Monkeys are primates with large brains. Unlike apes (gorillas, chimpanzees, orangutans, and gibbons), they have tails and relatively long backs. All, with the exception of baboons, have flattened faces, often without fur, that resemble human faces. Their eyes face forward, giving them excellent binocular vision for judging speed and distance when leaping through the trees. They also have good color vision, so they can spot flowering or fruiting trees from a distance.

Often the only large animals high in the canopy, monkeys are well adapted for life in the trees. Like humans, they have hands that can grasp objects or branches; many monkeys also have opposable big toes. Also like humans, they usually have flat nails on their fingers and toes and sensitive pads for touching and gripping. They walk on all fours, even on branches.

Many Central and South American monkeys use their long tail like a fifth limb. The tail can curl around branches and may have a bare, ridged pad under its tip, just like a finger pad, for extra friction in its grip. It is not uncommon to see a spider monkey hanging from a branch by its tail while it stretches out to reach a juicy fruit.

KEY FACTS

● **In Malaysia people train pig-tailed macaques to climb palm trees and pick coconuts.**

● **The monkeys of the Americas have broad noses with wide nostrils that face outward. Most African and Asian monkeys have narrower noses with nostrils that are close together and point downward.**

● **After a meal the contents of a colobus monkey's stomach will account for over a quarter of its body weight.**

● **DeBrazza's monkey, from Africa, is probably the most colorful monkey, with a black cap, orange forehead, blue spectacles, and a white beard.**

Enjoying the Feast

Some monkeys, such as the capuchins of Central and South America, eat almost everything, from tough leaves to fruits, flowers, gum, fungi, insects, spiders, frogs, lizards, eggs, baby birds, and even other monkeys. They use their hands to forage, tear open fruits

A douc langur monkey from Southeast Asia; its diet consists of fruit and leaves.

385

The Proboscis Monkey

One of the strangest inhabitants of the mangrove swamps of Borneo is the proboscis (pruh-BAH-suhs) monkey. Male proboscis monkeys have huge, bulbous noses, which they straighten out to make loud, honking sounds. They use their large tails for balancing as they leap from tree to tree. Proboscis monkeys feed on the shoots of mangroves and pedada trees and on flowers and fruits. They can often be seen sunbathing at the edge of the swamp.

a flowering or fruiting tree. Monkeys are important pollinators of canopy flowers: as they feed on the flowers, pollen sticks to their fur and rubs off on the next flower. They also help to disperse the seeds inside certain fruits. The monkeys eat the fruits, and the seeds pass out unharmed in their droppings.

Tough Meals

Plant fibers are difficult to digest. The leaf-eating colobus monkeys of Africa and the leaf monkeys and langurs of Asia have special pouches in their stomachs, like cows do. These pouches contain bacteria that can break down the plant fibers and produce food that the monkeys can absorb. Howler monkeys have bacteria in the other end of their gut, in the colon (large intestine) and a pouch called the cecum.

Macaques, mangabeys, mandrills, and guenons have cheek pouches. If they are feeding in exposed places where a large eagle or forest hawk might attack them, they cram their cheeks with leaves, then retreat to a more sheltered place to eat.

or bash them open against tree trunks, and explore cracks in tree bark in search of insects. The rain forest provides these foods all year round.

Monkeys forage in troops that differ in number and hierarchy with each species; many pairs of eyes are more likely to spot

Leaves do not provide much energy, so leaf-eating monkeys move slowly and forage over only a small area, spending about half the day sleeping. Because they can cope with the tough diet of leaves, they avoid competition with other monkeys over food.

Food for All

By feeding on different things and at different levels in the forest, up to five different species of monkeys can live in the same area and even feed in the same tree. Squirrel monkeys of Central and South America feed mainly on fruits and insects, while the howler monkeys in the same forests eat mostly leaves. Uakaris avoid competition by keeping to the unpopular swamp forests. Titi monkeys can eat unripe fruit, while the tiny marmosets are specialists in feeding on gum and have chisel-like front teeth to gouge holes in tree bark.

In western Africa red colobus monkeys feed high in the canopy on young leaf shoots and flowers, while black colobuses eat only mature leaves. The guenons eat unripe fruit. Mangabeys have sharp front teeth and can break into nuts and tough fruits. Mandrills eat almost all parts of plants but keep to the forest floor and low shrubs.

Raising Young

Like humans, most monkeys produce only one young at a time, but some of the smaller species, such as tamarins and marmosets, may give birth to twins. Young monkeys spend a long time with their mothers, learning how to catch insects, where to find food and water in their home territory, which foods are good to eat and which are bad-tasting or poisonous, and which are the safest routes through the forest. In many species most members of the troop help raise the young, carrying them, baby-sitting them, and bringing the mother food.

Play is extremely important to young monkeys. As they wrestle, jump, pounce, and chase each other, they are learning how to dodge enemies; the males are learning how to fight rivals in order to win females in later life. They become agile enough to catch insects and other prey

The male mandrill has a very dramatic face. Its rump, too, is bright blue or purple. Competition for mates is fierce, and calls for a big show of strength and color.

This Kenyan colobus monkey is a leaf-eater. It has large salivary glands and a large stomach containing bacteria that break down leaf fibers.

large owls to prey on small monkeys at night but plenty of large eagles and hawks around in the daytime. By feeding at night, the night monkey also avoids competition with other kinds of monkeys. The night monkey has huge eyes for seeing in dim light and is sometimes called the owl monkey. Its white face can easily be seen in the dark.

Night monkeys live in small groups, hiding by day in hollow trees. When feeding, they can be very noisy; their hooting calls (made at a rate of 10 to 30 hoots a minute) can be heard 550 yards (500 m) away. In more open areas where great horned owls are common and large eagles rare, night monkeys feed more in the daytime.

and develop the skills needed to leap from branch to branch. At the same time, they are learning their place in the troop— which individuals they can dominate and which ones they must respect.

Fortunately, as well as having a long childhood, monkeys also have a long life. They can breed at any time of year, so if a baby dies, its mother can mate and become pregnant again quickly.

Night Monkeys

Only one species of monkey is entirely nocturnal: the night monkey, or douroucouli (duhr-uh-KOO-lee), of South America. In the rain forest, there are a few

IN FOCUS

Sacred Monkeys

The rhesus monkey, or rhesus macaque (muh-KAK), lives in southern Asia. In some parts of India, it is believed to be a sacred animal and is common around both Buddhist and Hindu temples, where food may be put out for it. It feeds on fruits, seeds, roots, and insects.

Check these out:

- Canopy ● Communication ● Ecosystem
- Feeding ● Herbivore ● Mammal
- Marmoset and Tamarin ● Nocturnal
Animal ● Primate

Monsoon Rain Forest

A seasonal type of woodland called monsoon forest covers large areas of southern Asia, from central India to southeast China and northern Thailand. Temperatures in monsoon forests are much higher than those of rain forests, although nighttime frost is common in many monsoon forests during winter. The dry season in a monsoon forest can last as long as six months; it is followed by a prolonged period of rain that tends to arrive suddenly and then deluge the countryside for days or even weeks on end. Because of the prolonged absence of rainfall, many animals can breed only during part of the year, and creatures such as insects largely disappear during the drought. Thus the dry season makes for wildlife that is much less varied than that in the almost permanently wet rain forests.

Waiting for the Rains

In India the monsoon rains are eagerly awaited everywhere, bringing new life both to the overheated patchwork of rice fields and to the tinder-dry forests. Everyone and everything waits for rain, and the atmosphere is hot and tense, prickly with expectation. The main Indian monsoon comes from March to July and is the cue for an outburst of frenzied activity. Insects by the millions appear as if by magic a few days after the first drenching rains. With so much food so instantly available, the birds begin to cash in on the bonanza of insect life and start their hectic breeding season. Millions of leeches emerge from their dry-season hiding places. Famished after their long fast, they are eager to suck the blood of any warm-blooded creature within reach, including humans.

Plants of the Monsoon Forests

The trees in monsoon forests are generally much shorter and slimmer than in rain forests and seldom have buttressed roots. Teak, a valuable timber tree, is a

As in all monsoon forests, there is a long dry season in India's Periyar National Park. It is a haven for elephants and other large mammals.

common sight in the monsoon forest, along with the pines and casuarina trees that are absent from rain forests. Mountain ebony, nutmeg with its fragrant fruits, mahoganies, Indian rosewood, and the sandalwood tree are other typical inhabitants. At the end of the dry season, many of the trees come into flower. The flame-of-the-forest tree produces sensational sunbursts of orange as blossoms drench the bare twigs.

The monsoon forests at the base of the Himalayas get more rainfall than most, nurturing a dense forest of short, stout trees, such as cinnamon, magnolia, chestnut, birch, and plum, all heavily festooned with mosses and orchids. The best undisturbed areas of monsoon forest still remaining in Asia lie in the hilly, remote border region between Thailand and Myanmar. There, 80 percent or more of the annual rainfall comes in the monsoon months of May to October.

The spectacular orange flowers of the flame-of-the-forest tree appear at the end of the dry season in a number of India's national parks.

Animals of the Monsoon Forest

Even though the monsoon forests are poorer in insect species than the rain forests, they can support many larger animals. These include

elephants, sambar and spotted deer, nilgai antelope, leopards, tigers, and many kinds of squirrels. One area in Thailand has 10 kinds of primates and no fewer than 21 species of woodpeckers, the largest number for any similar-sized area in the world. This same forest is also home to the stump-tailed macaque. This monkey spends much of its time on the ground and has a virtually bald bright pink face with a bluish muzzle. The gaur, largest of Asia's wild cattle, is also found in monsoon forests. In India many of the most biodiverse monsoon forests are protected as national parks or reserves.

IN FOCUS

The Bonnet Macaque

Unlike many animals, the bonnet macaque (muh-KAK) is adaptable enough to flourish when the monsoon forest is disturbed or destroyed. It has survived with great success in the farms and towns that so often replace its native forests. It is named after the double tuft of hair on its head, divided by a central parting. The bonnet macaque's favorite food is figs.

Check these out:

- Asia
- Climate and Weather
- Rain Forest
- Season

Mosquito

There are more than 2,500 known species of mosquitoes, of which about 2,000 live in the tropical and subtropical parts of the world. Mosquitoes are small flies whose females generally need a meal of blood before they can lay their eggs. They get blood by sinking their needlelike mouthparts into any of a wide range of animals, including frogs, birds, monkeys, and people. They also suck nectar from flowers. Male mosquitoes have large, bushy antennae, with which they pick up the whining sound of the females when tracking them down for mating.

Life Cycle

After mating, the females lay their eggs singly or in little rafts on the surface of still water. The eggs hatch within a day or two, and the larvae that emerge are like wriggly tadpoles with large round heads. When disturbed, they squirm down into the water, but usually they spend most of their time hanging from the surface. They feed on microscopic organisms swept into their mouth by a fan of bristles on each side of their head. To breathe air, they break the water surface with a tiny tube at the rear end of their body. The larvae are fully grown in a few days and then turn into comma-shaped pupae. A few days later, adult mosquitoes break out of the pupae.

Huge numbers of mosquitoes breed in the rain forests in stagnant backwaters and also high in the canopy, where the larvae live in bromeliads (broe-MEE-lee-ads) and in tree holes. Many adults stay up there and take blood from birds and monkeys. These canopy-living species tend to be active at around sunset, although each species feeds at a slightly different time. Lower down in the forest, mosquito activity is spread more evenly throughout the day.

Carrying Disease

Female mosquitoes carry several serious human diseases, including malaria and yellow fever. The insects infect people when they take blood. During the 1880s malaria and yellow fever killed over 20,000 people building the Panama Canal. The canal could not be completed until biologists worked out how to control the disease-carrying mosquitoes decades later—by destroying their marshy breeding sites.

The beak projecting from the head of this female mosquito encloses her sharp blood-sucking equipment. After a meal of blood her body will become quite fat.

Check these out:
● Disease ● Mining ● Parasite

osses are small, flowerless plants with no real roots. Simple hairlike threads at the base anchor the plants to the ground or to other surfaces and soak up water and dissolved minerals. The leaves are small and delicate, with or without a central rib, and they absorb most of the water needed by the plants. Leaves usually cluster tightly around the stems. The stems are very slender, rarely more than a few centimeters long. The plants usually form dense cushions or carpets.

KEY FACTS

● **There are about 15,000 different kinds of mosses.**

● **In some high-altitude rain forests, the covering of mosses and liverworts is up to 12 in. (30 cm) thick on the oldest trunks and branches.**

Moss Reproduction

Although many mosses can survive dry weather, they reproduce only in damp conditions. Mosses reproduce by scattering dustlike spores instead of seeds. The microscopic spores are produced in capsules carried on slender, wiry stalks rising from the tips of some of the stems. These capsules are pear-shaped or cylindrical, and each is equipped with a detachable lid. When the lid falls, it reveals a number of slits or pores through which the spores can escape like pepper being shaken from a pepper shaker. When a spore reaches a suitably damp habitat, it grows into a slender, branching thread that creeps over the surface. Clusters of new moss stems then sprout from this thread.

The trees in this temperate rain forest in Washington's Olympic National Park are literally dripping with long, mossy garlands. Only a very wet climate can support such a rich growth of moss.

Water droplets cover moss in Costa Rica's rain forest.

Liverworts are closely related to mosses, but they have simple, spherical spore capsules that split wide open when ripe and release all their spores at once. The capsule stalks are always pale and fleshy. Liverwort leaves do not have a central rib. Most of them have toothed edges. Some liverworts have no leaves or stems; they look like green seaweed creeping over the ground.

Tropical Mosses

Mosses are most abundant in damp places, especially in the Tropics, but many species can also survive prolonged drought by holding water among their tightly packed leafy stems. Common in all kinds of woodlands, mosses grow on tree trunks and branches as well as on the ground. They form extensive carpets in many temperate forests, but they are less common on the dim floor of the rain forest. Most of the rain forest mosses grow among the ferns and other epiphytes on the trunks and branches. A few mosses even grow on leaves.

Epiphytic mosses grow mainly on the older tree trunks, where the bark is usually rougher and gives the plants a better footing. Relatively few mosses grow on slender young trees with smooth bark. The mosses growing on shaded trunks and branches below the canopy are often called shade epiphytes. Some of their stems are over 3 feet (1 m) long, and they often hang from the branches like garlands. Their leaves tend to be larger but thinner than those of other mosses. Some mosses grow high in the canopy, and they are often called sun epiphytes. Hanging species are usually rare in the canopy, where most of the mosses form compact mats or cushions. Their leaves are smaller and tougher than those of the shade epiphytes, since they have to withstand the drying effects of both sun and wind.

IN FOCUS

Mossy Forests

Rain forests growing more than about 3,000 ft. (900 m) above sea level are particularly rich in mosses, and some are called mossy forests because mosses and the very similar liverworts completely smother the trees and many of the lianas (lee-AH-nuhs), or woody vines. In fact the liverworts are usually more common than the mosses. The covering of mosses and liverworts is up to 12 in. (30 cm) thick on the oldest trunks and branches; it forms an excellent seedbed where orchids and other epiphytic plants can establish themselves.

Check these out:
● **Epiphyte** ● **Leaf** ● **Plant**

Mudskipper

Mudskippers are little fish that live like amphibians, spending part of their life in water and part on land. They can walk, skip, and even climb trees. When out of the water, they prop themselves up on their front fins, which are stiffened with bone and have joints resembling elbows. On some mudskippers the rear fins join together to form a sucker to help the fish cling to the aerial roots of the mangrove trees.

Like crabs, mudskippers keep their gill chambers full of water, returning to the sea to replenish them from time to time. They also take in oxygen from the air through their moist skins.

Six different species of mudskipper live in the mangrove swamps, estuaries, and mudflats of the Tropics and subtropics from the coasts of Africa to Australia and the Pacific Ocean. The largest mudskippers grow up to 12 inches (30 cm) long.

The smallest mudskippers live in shoals near the water's edge. They spend a lot of time in the water or wriggling through wet mud in search of tiny worms and shellfish. Mudskippers living up among the mangroves also feed on crabs, but the mudskippers in the middle of the mudflat are mainly vegetarians, grazing on algae.

Mudskippers live alone in burrows in the mud and defend territories several yards in diameter. A mudskipper may build a wall of mud around its territory to create a small pool and keep out neighbors. If another mudskipper ventures too close, the owner will dash out and confront it, raising the two brilliantly colored fins on its back and bobbing its head up and down. The male uses a similar display to attract females.

Mudskippers living near the low tide allow their young to be swept out to sea. The bigger mudskippers rear their young in the male's burrow at the bottom of his pool. The eggs and young remain there until the baby fish are well developed.

A mudskipper uses its stiff, muscular fins like little legs, skittering across the mud of mangrove swamps. Its large eyes are adapted for seeing in air, not water.

Check these out:
● Fish ● Mangrove Forest

National Park

Hundreds of national parks have been established in the rain forests of the world. The biggest of them are up to 10,000 square miles (26,000 km²) in extent. The purpose of most parks is to preserve areas that represent particular types of forest, especially those with exceptional levels of biodiversity. Unfortunately many of the forests with the most biodiversity lie in the lowlands, where farming and other commercial activities tend to have divided the forests into smaller pieces, destroying most of the forest and thus animals' habitats. Therefore most national parks have been created in more mountainous areas, leaving the rich lowland forests poorly represented. Since many of the larger mammals—such as elephants, tapirs, and rhinoceroses—are found mainly in lowland forests, these highland national parks are seldom adequate to protect them.

Some parks suffer from high levels of human presence around the edges; this suffering is compounded when people poach the animals for food, cut trees for firewood, and damage the parks in other ways. Such parks will work only if there is enough money for training an adequate number of staff to police the area to keep out unwanted intruders; for many poorer countries, setting aside these funds is difficult. Sometimes countries prefer to establish a park that has a completely undisturbed core area, dedicated to wildlife conservation in its purest sense. This is surrounded by a so-called buffer zone of forest that absorbs the human impact of the people who use it.

Many parks exist on paper only, and no rangers protect the area. Even parks that are well staffed often fail because rangers are poorly paid and have little or no

KEY FACTS

● **Korup National Park contains one-fourth of all Africa's known primate species.**

● **Costa Rica has set aside about 25 percent of its land area for national parks and reserves.**

● **The Royal Nepalese Army had to be brought in to protect the rhinoceroses from poachers in Chitwan National Park.**

● **Access to many South American parks is by riverboat only.**

Khao Yai National Park in Thailand is renowned both for its wildlife and for its many waterfalls.

training. Sometimes staff are actually a part of the problem, killing and eating the animals they are supposed to protect. Governments often do not even guarantee to preserve their parks, and development has destroyed many parks when the government has decided to put farming interests above conservation.

Improving Parks

In many countries the situation is improving as governments discover the financial value of their parks: parks bring in tourists; tourists spend money. The cash earned from a constant flow of visitors may be far more than could be gained from logging or farming. In addition, the income from tourism brings in highly prized foreign currency year after year.

Many recent projects aim to closely involve local people in preserving the park by offering a percentage of the entrance fees paid by visitors. The Kuna Indian Forest Park in Panama is dedicated to preserving the ancestral forests as a national park, and the Indians receive a steady income from fees paid by visiting scientists and tourists. Similar projects are also in place in Ecuador and

IN FOCUS

Ranomafana

The best rain forest national park in Madagascar is probably Ranomafana, which has one of the highest primate species counts in the world, with no fewer than 12 different types of lemurs (LEE-muhrs). These include two of the rarest, the gray bamboo lemur and the golden bamboo lemur. Most of the lemurs are quite easy to view at close range, since many of them are accustomed to seeing people and have been studied for long periods by scientists.

Taman Negara National Park in Malaysia is a paradise for birdwatchers, although rain forest birds can be quite tricky to spot.

possible in some Indian parks, while Chitwan in Nepal offers easy views of the rare Indian one-horned rhinoceros. In southern India the most heavily visited reserve is Periyar, which receives more than 150,000 people a year. Large herds of elephants are often seen coming out of the forest to feed and drink, and there are packs of the increasingly scarce Indian wild dog. The large and striking Malabar squirrel feeds in the forest around the park's main hotel, and brilliantly colored birds fly everywhere. Armed guards regularly patrol the forest for poachers and wood collectors.

In Thailand the most visited park is Khao Yai, which is only about 100 miles (160 km) from Bangkok. The park lies in a mountain range, and one of its most important functions is to preserve the watershed and safeguard the water supply for the nearby cities. (Watershed protection is one of the main reasons for the existence of many national parks, such as Guatopo in Venezuela and Kerinci in Indonesia.) Khao Yai protects one of the largest remaining intact areas of dry evergreen and semievergreen rain forest on the Asian mainland. It is a birdwatcher's paradise, with over 300 species of birds, many of them dazzlingly beautiful, such as the scarlet minivet and Asian fairy bluebird. The 20 or more species of large mammals include the Asiatic black bear, elephant, and tiger, along with a wide range of primates.

One of Asia's finest parks is Taman Negara in Malaysia, which protects a large area of one of the world's oldest lowland tropical rain forests. The park is home to

several other countries. Local villagers are also encouraged to act as guides within some parks and may even receive specialist training in other countries in conservation work.

Establishing a decent level of facilities for tourists is now the top priority in many parks as people realize the value of eco-tourism. Parks now provide rooms for tourists, often consisting of attractive wooden buildings with thatched roofs. Generators or solar panels usually provide electricity, although in some parks kerosene lamps light the way. Some parks, even in remote areas such as Amazonia, have amazingly good facilities, with iced beverages constantly on offer to ease the discomfort of the heat and humidity.

Asian National Parks

National parks have been established in most forest types in Asia, including monsoon forests, mountain forests, dwarf coastal forests, and lowland rain forests. Tiger spotting from elephant back is

200 to 400 Negrito aboriginal people, who still live by hunting and harvesting forest products in the traditional manner of their ancestors. Access to the park is an adventure in itself, involving a three-hour trip upriver by boat. Within the park are hundreds of miles of walking trails, but the forest is very dense, making animals difficult to see. The best views are often to be had from blinds placed near salt licks, where tapirs come to feed.

African Parks

At present one of the best places to see a cross section of African rain forest wildlife is in Uganda, which has emerged from a long period of internal strife and is racing ahead economically. This economic success has enabled the Ugandan government to establish a system of well-managed rain forest parks that are attracting increasing numbers of foreign tourists. In Kibale forest visitors can track

In many national parks, such as here in Brunei on the island of Borneo, foreign scientists work alongside local forest officers to catalog the area's plant life.

chimpanzees or try spotting spectacular black-and-white colobus, red colobus, and other monkeys, plus a wealth of bird life and insects. Tourists must take guides when walking through the forest as part of the plan to benefit the country's economy by hiring local people.

Several superb national parks in Ivory Coast, Nigeria, and Cameroon protect some of the most diverse remaining areas of western Africa's rain forest. The Korup National Park in Cameroon is probably the most famous of these, covering 900 square miles (2,330 km²) of some of the best remaining equatorial rain forest in Africa. It is rich in primates, including chimpanzees, and also contains more than 400 species of trees. An ongoing program researches the medicinal properties of all

Lamington National Park

Northeastern Australia contains a scattering of rain forest national parks that, between them, contain an amazingly high percentage of the country's unique plant and animal life. One of the most popular areas is Lamington National Park, an area of subtropical rain forest and adjacent dry forest with an extensive network of walking trails. The park contains hundreds of species of orchids and many kinds of birds and animals. Some of these, including possums and sugar gliders (flying possums), are very tame. Tameness reaches an extreme in the spectacular crimson rosella parrots, which will steal the food from a person's hand as they raise it to their mouth. The bowerbirds are almost as tame, while at night tourists may be serenaded by groups of male Australian red-eyed leaf frogs, which pump out their amazingly loud songs from bulbous yellow throat sacs.

the forest's diverse plant life. As with many of the more progressive parks, the management of Korup involves close cooperation with the local people, who continue their traditional hunting and gathering activities in part of the reserve allocated for this. The pride and joy of the Cross River National Park in Nigeria is the population of western lowland gorillas, which were only recently discovered there after

having been thought long extinct in the region.

Parks in the Americas

In North America the most famous of the rain forest parks is the Olympic National Park in Washington State, which contains the Hoh rain forest. With a year-round rainfall averaging 145 inches (3,700 mm), it is not surprising that the ancient trees are densely felted with a growth of mosses and lichens. Elks, beavers, otters, and flying squirrels inhabit the forest. A visitors' center with interpretive displays helps the nonexpert understand what the forest is all about and how it works, and a good system of trails allows visitors to enjoy the wilderness.

Many of South America's parks are huge, although tourist facilities are often absent and real protection for the park is limited or even nonexistent. The most famous park, and one of the largest, is Manú in Peru's Amazonian lowlands.

Before tracking gorillas in Uganda's Bwindi National Park, tourists are briefed on what to do in the forest.

These tourists standing beside a giant buttressed tree are enjoying the thrill of being in one of the world's last great wildernesses, Manú National Park in Peru.

IN FOCUS

La Amistad

The Central American country with the best-known and most-visited rain forest parks is Costa Rica, which is now a popular center for eco-tourism. The biggest park there, La Amistad (meaning "friendship"), is shared with neighboring Panama and is quite remote. The park protects the highest biodiversity in the country in a huge variety of ecosystems. The great differences in altitude and geography within the park, from Costa Rica's highest mountain to steamy lowland rain forest, help create this variety. La Amistad contains more than 215 species of mammals, and among its 560 or so birds is the magnificent red-and-green resplendent quetzal (ket-SAHL), one of the most spectacular birds in the world.

Its 5,900 square miles (15,300 km²) of pristine lowland rain forest is home to an amazingly wide variety of fauna and flora. The park is divided into three zones: a Culture Zone where local people can still live off the forest, a much larger Reserve Zone used for eco-tourism, and a very much bigger core area, Park Zone, reserved for biologists conducting wildlife research. The best-studied of the park's animals are its 13 different species of primates, one of the highest primate counts in the world for a given area. The dense forest is home to over 1,000 species of birds, including flocks of parrots and macaws that throng on a riverbank clay lick.

Check these out:

- Africa
- Asia
- Australia
- Careers
- Central America
- Congo
- Conservation
- Exploration and Research
- Indonesia
- Kuna People
- Madagascar
- North America
- Oil Exploration
- Poaching
- Rain Forest
- South America
- Tourism

atural selection is the way in which animals and plants change gradually over time as a result of certain of their offspring surviving and adapting better than others. The great advantage of sexual reproduction, as practiced by most plants and animals, is that the offspring are not identical copies of one parent. Every single seedling produced by a tree or caterpillar produced by a butterfly is slightly different from another and from its parents. This means that not all offspring have an equal chance of survival. Some individuals have characteristics that give them a special advantage in life. These are more likely to survive and to pass on any advantages they possess to their offspring.

The tropical rain forests have produced more species of plants and animals than any other kind of habitat on Earth; all of them have been produced by the process of natural selection. Thousands of seedlings germinate each year from many rain forest trees, yet only a few will ever survive to produce a mature tree that will produce seeds of its own. Many of the seedlings die, maybe because they are on the wrong type of soil, but any individuals that are less sensitive to soil type might survive and prosper. Another decisive factor in survival might be the ability to grow fast and reach the canopy first. However, some of the slower-growing trees might have invested some of their energy in producing some unusual chemical that will defend them against insect attack. This could then give them an advantage over faster-growing trees, whose leaves get eaten before they are even half grown, allowing the chemically protected slowpokes to overtake them.

KEY FACTS

● **Many rain forest insects and spiders look like bird droppings.**

● **Some insects lay thousands of eggs, but on average only a few will survive to produce adults.**

● **Natural selection has produced some surprising results, such as the huge beak of the toucan and the long arms of the gibbon.**

Physical Variations

Among the animals of the forest, natural selection has produced some surprising results, such as the huge beak of the toucan, the long arms of the gibbon, and the weird,

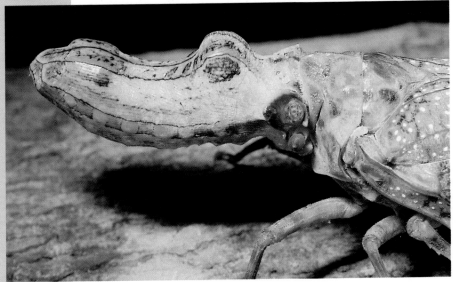

The puzzlingly inflated head of the peanut bug is an example of natural selection.

Charles Darwin

Charles Darwin, an Englishman (1809–1882), was one of the greatest naturalists who ever lived. After a trip to South America and the Pacific as a naturalist on the sailing ship HMS *Beagle*, Darwin proposed his revolutionary theory of evolution based on natural selection. His brilliantly original ideas on this subject arose mainly from his observations of finches in the Galápagos Islands, far off the coast of Ecuador. Another naturalist, Alfred Russel Wallace, independently reached the same conclusions as Darwin, so both men published their new theory jointly at a meeting of the Linnaean Society in London in 1858.

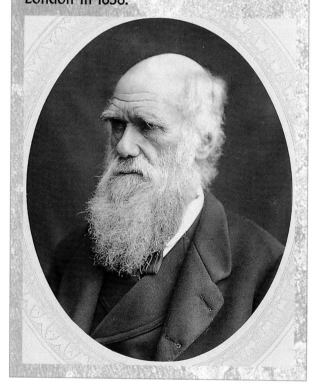

inflated head of the peanut bug. The development of all these features has given the animal some advantage, such as feeding on hard fruits for the toucan or moving swiftly through the treetops for the gibbon. People once thought that the peanut bug was an exception, as natural selection had produced a conspicuous feature—the peanut-shaped head—that seemed to have no obvious advantage to its possessor and appeared to be a clumsy hindrance in its daily life. Scientists now think that the head imitates a lizard's head—which may scare off some predators.

Camouflage and Mimicry

The most impressive examples of natural selection in the rain forests can be seen in the many different strategies of camouflage and mimicry evolved by the insects. If one member of a group of katydid offspring produces an adult that looks more like a leaf than the others, then that adult is more likely to survive and reproduce. The slow process of natural selection's weeding out ensures that what starts out to be vaguely leaflike ends up being a perfect imitation of a leaf. Through the continuous processes of natural selection, leaf-mimicking grasshoppers, mantises, cockroaches, butterflies, moths, bugs, beetles, spiders, fish, frogs, and lizards have all gone down the same evolutionary road.

Natural selection has produced a variety of rain forest insects and spiders that look like bird droppings, which are of no interest to predators such as birds or monkeys. The most remarkable example is a katydid nymph from South America. To be absolutely convincing, the nymph sits with its legs splayed out flat against a leaf, resembling a fresh dropping.

Check these out:
- Butterfly and Moth ● Camouflage
- Evolution of the Rain Forest
- Grasshopper, Cricket, and Katydid
- Mantis

Nest and Nest Building

Nests serve many purposes. In temperate regions many animals live year-round in well-lined nests that keep them warm. However, keeping warm in the Tropics is usually not a problem; the main purpose of nests in the rain forest is to shelter young animals. The soft lining of some nests helps protect and cushion the delicate babies from the hard earth of burrows or the rough interiors of tree hollows. The nests of birds and squirrels also conceal the young from the eyes of predators such as forest hawks and eagles.

KEY FACTS

● **Crowned eagles do not build fresh nests for each new brood they rear. Instead they add a new layer to their existing nest.**

● **Oropendolas often build their nests alongside wasp nests. The wasps attack animals coming to raid the oropendola nests, while the oropendolas drive off caracaras (hawks) that attack the wasps.**

● **The male paradise fish from Indonesia builds a large bubble nest at the water's surface or under a floating leaf. The female lays her eggs under this nest, and they float up into it.**

Miniature Cities

The nests sheltering the young of many social insects, such as bees, wasps, ants, and termites, are like miniature cities, sometimes with many chambers for different purposes and covered walkways leading out into the forest. Even the tiny stingless bees that are so common in tropical rain forests build nests with many chambers. Tiny, upside-down cups made of about a dozen hexagonal (six-sided) cells are suspended from a leaf by a little stalk. In these cells the bees rear their young. Bees build their nests from flakes of wax produced in special glands on their bellies, often mixed with plant resins.

Paper wasps make communal nests of papery material made from chewed bits of wood. Other wasps, such as potter wasps, live alone and make urn-shaped nests of mud for their eggs and young; they may stock them with paralyzed insects or spiders as food for their offspring.

The forest floor, tree trunks, branches, and even the underside of large leaves are home to termites. Termite nests are made of carton, which is like cardboard that is made from chewed wood mixed with saliva. The simplest termite nests are just caves, spherical carton structures wrapped around twigs or

A colony of nocturnal wasps dangles from a branch in the Amazon rain forest. The nest comprises many individual cells in which the wasps' larvae are reared.

branches. Some tree-dwelling termites make large hanging nests with many chambers and passages. Covered tunnels lead down the tree to favorite foraging areas, the carton protecting the termites from the gaze of birds and other predators.

Termites living on the forest floor have some of the most spectacular nests, with underground cellars, nurseries, pantries with food, a royal chamber for the king and queen, and aboveground towers that serve as part of the air-conditioning system. Inside the termite nest, water is

A chestnut-headed oropendola from Panama stands on her extraordinary nest. Such suspended nests are difficult for many predators to reach.

IN FOCUS

Bubble Nests

Some frogs, such as the South American foam nest frogs, make frothy nests of bubbles of air and mucus at the water's surface or on damp ground near water. When they hatch, the tadpoles will make their way to the nearest water. Nobody knows the advantage of this kind of nest. Perhaps it is distasteful to predators, or the white mass of foam may reflect heat so that the nest stays moist longer.

drawn up from cellars deep below ground and passes along special tunnels to the surface of the tower, where it evaporates, cooling the air and drawing more moist air through the nest.

Woven Nests

Bird nests are simple when compared to the nests of most social insects, but they come in many different forms and are built of many different materials, such as leaves, twigs, feathers, lichens, spiderwebs, mud, and saliva. Some South American hummingbirds make tiny nests of spiderwebs suspended on fine, leafy strips from the tips of large leaves. Holding the end of a thread of spider's web, they fly around the nest, draping it in silk.

The tailorbirds of Southeast Asia use spider silk differently. They pull leaves together to form a cup to hold their nest, then pierce holes in them. Using their beaks like needles, they pull strands of spider silk, cottonlike threads from seeds, or fibers from tree bark through the holes, twisting them into a knot on the other side to hold the stitch.

Other birds weave intricate nests from sticks, grasses, leaves, and other materials, lining them with soft feathers, grasses, lichens, and spiderwebs. Some of the most complex nests are those of the oropendolas of Central and South America. Their teardrop-shaped nests hang on long woven strings from the branches of trees, where most predators cannot reach them. Oropendolas often build their nests alongside wasp nests. The wasps attack possums or snakes coming to raid the oropendola nests, while the oropendolas drive off caracaras (hawks) that might attack the wasp nest.

Birds are not the only animal weavers. The weaver ants of Asia fold over leaves to create chambers, gluing them together with sticky silk produced by their larvae. The ants pass the larvae back and forth like shuttles in a loom as they glue the leaves together.

Homes of Mud and Muck
Some birds have sticky saliva that acts like glue. Swifts, found throughout the Tropics, stick twigs, moss, and feathers together to make their nests, which they glue to the inside of hollow trees or cracks in rocks. The Asian palm swift will make a tiny nest of feathers on the surface of a dangling palm leaf, then glue its eggs to the nest.

Some birds build their homes from pellets of mud mixed with straw and cow droppings. This mud sets hard as it dries. Ovenbirds, found throughout the tropical Americas, build their nests on tree stumps or other objects. The nest is a closed chamber with an entrance shielded from the outside by another internal wall so that predators cannot simply put their paws inside.

In the rain forests of Australia, the rainbow pitta builds an ordinary nest, but its eggs are at serious risk from brown tree snakes, which detect the nests by their smell. Many pittas decorate their nests with wallaby droppings to disguise their scent.

The male birds of some species make nests purely for show. Females are attracted to the male with the best nest, a sign that he will provide for the young. Often, however, the female will build her own nest in which to rear her chicks.

Larger animals also build nests. Primates such as chimpanzees, gorillas, and orangutans build leafy platforms of twigs and branches on which to sleep. Crocodiles and caimans build mounds of rotting vegetation in which to lay their eggs. As the plant material rots, it gives off heat, which speeds up the development of the embryos inside.

A group of mountain gorillas resting. Gorillas make nests of twisted branches and leaves in which to sleep.

Check these out:
● Ant ● Bee and Wasp ● Bird ● Crocodile and Caiman ● Fish ● Frog and Toad ● Gorilla ● Hummingbird ● Termite

New Zealand

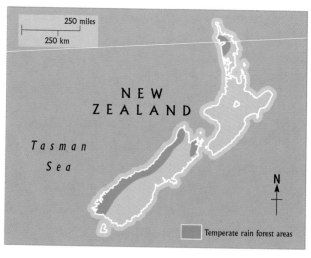

Before humans landed on and settled in New Zealand, forest covered much of the island. Maori settlers cleared some forests for farming land, and in more recent times white settlers cleared much more. About 35 percent of the original forest remains, composed mainly of different kinds of temperate rain forest. Most of the true rain forest lies in the western part of the country, where winds blowing in from the sea drop about 300 inches (7,500 mm) of rain each year. Indeed in some places as much as 10 inches (250 mm) of rain may fall in 24 hours. Where rainfall is too heavy, the soil is washed away, and not even rain forest is able to develop. Although a great deal of rain forest has been cut down, the New Zealand government has now set up a management project to protect most of what is left.

As in North America's rain forests, the main trees of the New Zealand rain forest are conifers. They are not, however, true pines, which they resemble, but

come from a different family called the podocarps. Known as pines, they include rimu, red pine, and matai, the black pine. Growing alongside these are broad-leaved trees including southern beeches and rata trees. The rata is to the New Zealand rain forest what the strangler fig is to tropical rain forests. It starts off climbing up another kind of tree but eventually grows all over the original tree, strangling it and leaving the rata standing on its own.

Of the rain forest animals in New Zealand perhaps the most familiar is that odd bird, the kiwi, which has its nostrils on the end of its beak and is wingless. Though domestic cats, which were brought by settlers, have wiped them out in some areas, kiwis can still be found on the forest floor, poking around in search of their main food, earthworms. New Zealand originally had no small rodents such as mice; their place in the food web is occupied by giant crickets called wetas.

Tree ferns growing in Westland National Park in New Zealand's South Island.

Check these out:
● Locomotion ● Rain Forest
● Temperate Rain Forest

406

Nocturnal Animal

If all the animals in the rain forest went out to look for food at the same time, the forest would be a very crowded place—and there would be a lot of competition for food and space.

Animals that are active at night, nocturnal animals, experience a very different world than those active in the daytime—a world of sounds and smells rather than of sights. Since it is impossible to see color in dim light, nocturnal animals do not need to be camouflaged. Nor is it much use being brightly colored, though white markings on the face help animals recognize members of their group in dim light if they are not too far apart.

Cold-blooded animals cannot generate their own body heat but rely on absorbing heat from their surroundings to gain enough energy to keep active. Fortunately the rain forest is warm and humid both day and night, allowing cold-blooded animals, such as insects, reptiles, and amphibians, to be active at night.

At Dawn and Dusk

The busiest times of day in the rain forest are dawn and dusk. Deer, bats, and owls all emerge at dusk, and some come out again at dawn. Animals such as bats all emerge at the same time to reduce the chance that individuals will be snatched by predators. The ant- and termite-eating armadillos and anteaters of South and Central America and the pangolins of Africa and Asia are also on the move at this time, relying mainly on their sense of smell to find their prey.

Some rain forest plants are also nocturnal.

The night monkey, or douroucouli, of South America is the only nocturnal monkey in the world.

Remaining closed all day, moth-pollinated flowers open and start to produce nectar just before dusk.

As soon as the sun sets, a nightly chorus starts up. Crickets start to chirp, since there is less risk of being found by predators. Frogs too begin their chorus at dusk.

Many cats can see well in dim light: tigers, jaguars, and leopards hunt mainly at night, especially around dusk. In Australia the nocturnal spotted tail quoll or tiger cat and native cat have large ears and whiskers that are sensitive to touch as well as to vibrations in the air caused by nearby movement.

Supersight

Many animals can see in the dark—or at least in very dim light. What may appear totally dark to humans may only be dim to a nocturnal animal such as an owl or tiger. Large eyes can take in more light than small ones. Rain forest animals with huge eyes include galagos, aye-ayes, possums, South American night monkeys, slow-moving lorises, and owls.

IN FOCUS

Hunting with Heat

Some snakes, including pythons, boa constrictors, anacondas, and pit vipers, find their warm-blooded prey by body heat. They have small heat-sensing organs on their snout, each one opening to the skin surface through a tiny hole. The snakes analyze the difference between the heat detected by sensors on either side of their head to find the direction of the heat source, like seeing with heat. Each organ may contain up to 7,000 nerve endings and can detect changes as small as 0.0054°F (0.003°C).

Vertebrates' eyes use two kinds of light receptors—rods and cones. Rods cannot detect color, but they can see detail and light and shade, so they work well in dim light. Cones see color but give a less detailed picture. Nocturnal animals are often color-blind, as their eyes have mainly rods and few cones. Nocturnal fish, frogs, toads, snakes, mice, deer, caimans, and even spiders have a special glistening layer, the tapetum, at the back of the eye that reflects stray light back through the eye so that it is not wasted.

Noises in the Night

Noise is a good way of communicating in the dark. Many nocturnal animals have acute hearing, often aided by large ears. Galagos, for example, can turn their huge,

Although the slow loris has large eyes with good night vision, it uses its sense of smell to sniff out prey.

furless ears around to face the direction from which sound is coming and even fold them up when they sleep. With eardrums on the side of their body, moths can sometimes hear bats approaching and take action to avoid them.

Many birds have small, vibration-sensitive organs on their legs that pick up the tiny movements of the branch or ground as a predator approaches their roost. Spiders, cockroaches, and many other insects have similar sensors.

Many nocturnal hunters, such as cats and foxes, have sensitive hearing; foxes can detect an earthworm's bristles brushing against leaves. Owls hunt mainly by hearing, using eyesight only to avoid obstacles as they fly. The large facial disks of owls, formed from flattened feathers, act like the receiving dish of a radio telescope, collecting sounds and focusing them on the ears hidden at the side of the head.

Night predators must be as silent as possible when hunting. Owls' soft feathers with fine fringes muffle the sound of their wings. Their prey seldom hear them coming. Tigers and other cats have soft pads on their feet and can sneak up silently on their prey.

Instead of avoiding noise, bats use it to hunt, sending out high-pitched sounds above the range of human hearing and listening for the echoes as the sound bounces off objects in their path. As a bat homes in on an insect, it emits more and more rapid clicks to fine-tune its

The face of this sooty owl from New Guinea has large ovals of flattened feathers around its eyes which direct sounds into the ears.

positioning. Some bats have nose leaves, frills around their noses, that act like megaphones to amplify their squeaks.

Communicating with Scent

At night in the rain forest, the air is still, and scents can linger for a long time. The scents produced by plants and animals are really messages. Night-opening flowers attract animals with scent.

Animal scents give information about sex and species or readiness for mating— or simply about ownership of a territory. Animals such as foxes and mongooses scent mark throughout their territory.

The Net-Casting Spider

The net-casting spider, found in Australian tropical forests, hunts at night. Its huge eyes, adapted for night vision, are 19 times more sensitive to light than a human's. It spins a sling-shaped web, then hangs upside down just above the ground or above a leaf surface, holding its net between two claws. When an unsuspecting insect passes below, the spider flings its net over it.

Rats and mice also smear their trails with scent. Cats exude scent as they scratch tree trunks. Laying scent messages is much less risky than making noises that a predator might follow.

Mammals are scent experts. Their special message-giving scents are called pheromones. Some mammals release pheromones in their droppings or urine, often spraying bushes or rocks along their path. These scent trails tell other animals whose territory they are in and give other information about the owner.

Insects also use scent signals, with scent sensors in many parts of their bodies, especially their legs and feet. Male moths have highly branched antennae covered in scent-sensing hairs, up to 17,000 hairs on each one. These can detect the scent of a female moth over distances of more than two-thirds of a mile (1 km).

With Feeling

Nocturnal animals usually possess a particularly good sense of touch, which helps them avoid obstacles in dim light. Most invertebrates can sense if the ground or the air vibrates, which might mean a predator is close at hand. Insects have touch-sensitive hairs on their body, especially on their legs. Touch and taste sensors blanket their feelers, or antennae. Snails have touch sensors on their tentacles and in other parts of their bodies.

Feathers and fur are sensitive to touch. Many nocturnal mammals, such as shrews, also have extra-long, extra-sensitive hairs called vibrissae. Some birds have vibrissae, too. Owls and nightjars, for instance, have fans of whiskers around their beaks. Whiskers protect their eyes while they are flying and tell them when to blink to avoid flying insects.

Check these out:

Bat Butterfly and Moth Carnivore
Cave Centipede Civet Galago
Loris Owl Possum Snake

The North American rain forest grows along the West Coast in a narrow band between the sea and the inland mountain ranges. It stretches from the coastal ranges of California to southern Alaska. Though very fragmented in places as a result of clear-cutting, this rain forest is estimated to still cover about 78,000 square miles (200,000 km²).

The minimum amount of rain that falls each year is about 80 inches (2,000 mm), but as much as 167 inches (4,250 mm) may fall in some parts of the forest in some years. In a tropical rain forest, it rains at some time or another year-round. In the North American coastal forests, it rains primarily during the winter months, while the summers tend to be warm and

KEY FACTS

● **Two-thirds of today's remaining coastal rain forest stand in North America; the remainder is shared among New Zealand, southern Australia, and Chile.**

● **Unlike tropical rain forests where most trees are broad-leaved, in the North American temperate rain forest, the main tree species are conifers.**

● **Most temperate rain forest animals live on the forest floor.**

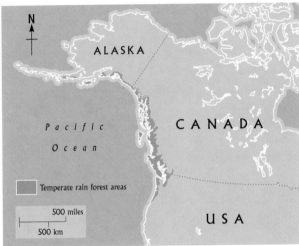

dry. During the summer the forest relies on sea fogs to provide most of the moisture. Temperature extremes are not as great as farther inland because the forest is protected from cold air coming off the land in winter by the mountains in the east and the sea, which never gets very cold, in the west.

Forest Composition
In the tropical rain forest grow scattered specimens of hundreds of different species of trees. In contrast temperate rain forests

The North American rain forest is dominated by conifers, beneath which grow many ferns and mosses.

411

The northern flying squirrel glides from tree to tree using the broad webs of skin between its front and back legs.

plants. It is difficult, however, for tree seeds to get enough light to grow beneath this thick layer of vegetation. Their best chance for success is to germinate on an old log, where they are up in the light, and send their roots over the log and into the soil. Eventually this "nurse log" rots away, leaving the tree to grow on its own.

Forest Animals

Unlike in tropical rain forests, where many of the animals live up in the sunlit leaf canopy, most of the temperate rain forest animals live on the forest floor. The trees do, however, provide a home and a source of food for many species of birds, including eagles, spotted and barred owls, and woodpeckers, as well as squirrels and the red-backed vole. The northern flying squirrel feeds on seeds and nuts but comes down to the ground to search for truffles, fungi that grow on tree roots. These squirrels do not fly but glide from tree to tree as far as 80 yards (73 m), using flaps of skin that stretch between the front and back legs along either side of their body.

Rivers, lakes, and ponds in the forest provide homes for ducks and geese, herons and kingfishers, and otters and mink. These last two no doubt feed in part on the salmon that come up the larger rivers to spawn in the smaller streams that run through the forest.

Larger animals also inhabit the forest. People have hunted the cougar, or mountain lion, for years, but its numbers are now increasing in the forests. Despite

contain many examples of a few types of trees. Two main types dominate the temperate rain forest, both conifers—the Sitka spruce and the western hemlock. Douglas fir, western red cedar, and a number of broad-leaved tree species occur in smaller numbers. Some of the dominant trees can grow to an enormous size, up to 300 feet (90 m) in height and 23 feet (7 m) around the base of the trunk. Another important difference between these forests and the tropical forests is that during the winter months most of the ground plants die back and the deciduous, broad-leaved trees all lose their leaves.

In temperate rain forests, a thick growth of mosses, lichens, and ferns covers tree trunks and competes for growing space on the ground with a variety of flowering

IN FOCUS

Conifers

A total of 19 species of conifers are found down the whole length of the forest from Alaska to northern California. A further 8 species grow only from southern Oregon southward, while 2 species are found just in the southern Oregon forest. This makes for 29 conifer species in the forest as a whole, an amazing statistic, since only 115 species grow in all of North America.

its large size—with a head and body length of up to 5 feet (1.5 m)—it often feeds on small animals such as grasshoppers and mice. However, it preys mainly on deer. Even bigger is the black bear. Mainly a plant eater, it will also feed on small animals, fish, and any carrion it finds. Two of the larger grazing animals found in the forest are the black-tailed deer and the elk, also known as the Roosevelt elk in this area.

Protecting the Forest

Established in 1938, Olympic National Park lies in Washington State on a peninsula west of Seattle, the state capital. Olympic National Park is where the largest area of untouched temperate rain forest in the Western Hemisphere—30,000 acres (12,150 hectares)— is preserved, and the park includes the largest uncut area of coniferous forest in the continuous 48 states.

The Roosevelt elk is one of the larger animals that live in the North American rain forest.

Check these out:
● Climate and Weather ● Owl ● Rain Forest ● Squirrel ● Temperate Rain Forest

The rain forest is one of the most productive habitats on Earth. In the warm, moist environment of the forest, plants grow incredibly fast, scrambling over each other to reach the light. The warmth and high humidity also suit the growth of fungi and bacteria, which rot dead plants and animals.

KEY FACTS

● **The mass of plant material above ground in a rain forest is some 160 tn. per acre (400 metric tons per ha).**

● **A large proportion of a rain forest's nutrients are locked up in the plants and animals and not in the soil.**

● **Carnivorous plants such as pitcher plants and bladderworts get extra nitrates by trapping insects.**

Rapid Recycling

Plants need many different nutrients, especially nitrates, phosphates, and potassium, and in smaller amounts magnesium, iron, sulfur, and many other substances. Plant roots absorb dissolved minerals from the soil, and the minerals combine with sugars made by photosynthesis in the leaves to form all the chemical compounds that make up the plant's body. The plants are eaten by animals, so they pass on

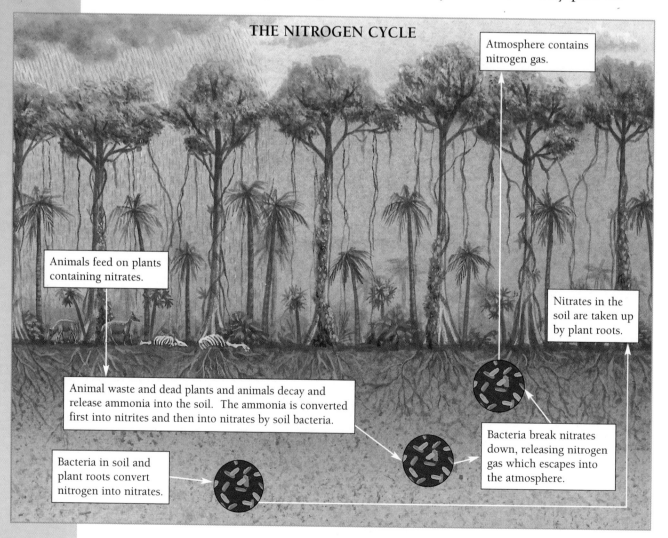

THE NITROGEN CYCLE

Atmosphere contains nitrogen gas.

Animals feed on plants containing nitrates.

Nitrates in the soil are taken up by plant roots.

Animal waste and dead plants and animals decay and release ammonia into the soil. The ammonia is converted first into nitrites and then into nitrates by soil bacteria.

Bacteria break nitrates down, releasing nitrogen gas which escapes into the atmosphere.

Bacteria in soil and plant roots convert nitrogen into nitrates.

Fungus Partners

Fungi don't just help to break down tissues and release nutrients; some fungi also help plants absorb nutrients. They live wrapped around roots or even inside roots, taking in nutrients from the soil faster than the plant can. The fungus benefits from sugars supplied by the plant. These plant-root partnerships are called mycorrhizae. Mycorrhizae have been found on some of the oldest plant fossils, dating back hundreds of millions of years. Most present-day forest trees and shrubs have mycorrhizae, and so do many orchids and equisetums, also known as horsetails.

their nutrients, and the animals are in turn food for other animals. A large proportion of a rain forest's nutrients are locked up in the plants and animals and not in the soil; the soils of many rain forests are actually quite thin.

Dead leaves, flowers, twigs, logs, and animals rot down quickly in tropical rain forests. Insects, such as wood-boring beetles and the larvae of flies and beetles, aid in decomposition, as do fungi (FUN-jie) and bacteria. The nutrients the decomposing matter once contained are released into the soil in the waste products of the decomposers, where they can be taken up once again by the roots of plants.

Capturing Nitrogen

Nitrogen is one of the most important elements for living things. Plant roots need to take in nitrogen as nitrates, soluble nitrogen compounds dissolved in groundwater. Some of these nitrates come from the rocks beneath the soil, released

as the rocks are broken down by heat and water, but some are formed from nitrogen in the air between soil particles by nitrogen-fixing bacteria.

Some plants, mainly those from the pea family, house nitrogen-fixing bacteria in their roots. The bacteria supply nitrates to the plant, and the plant in turn supplies the bacteria with sugars produced by photosynthesis, a mutually beneficial arrangement (called symbiosis).

Carnivorous plants such as pitcher plants and bladderworts get extra nitrates by trapping insects in various ways, digesting them or letting bacteria digest them, then absorbing the nitrates released by digestion. Other plants have special cavities inside their stems or leaf bases where ants make their nests. The ants' droppings and the decay of dead ants release nitrates for the plant.

Runaway Soil

Heavy rainfalls wash the Tropics. Without the forest to protect the soil, its nutrients would soon be swept away into the rivers. Instead, water trickles slowly through the dense vegetation and seeps, little by little, into the soil below. Plants absorb much of this water along the way.

When large areas of rain forest are cleared, the soil is unprotected; nutrients soon wash away. Crops are often not dense enough to protect the soil, and the soil quickly erodes, becoming infertile. Harvesting those crops removes many vital nutrients.

Check these out:
- Bacteria - Carnivorous Plant
- Decomposer - Erosion - Forest Floor
- Fungus - Lichen - Symbiosis

Oil Exploration

Oil is an important raw material for the world's industries. In its natural form, oil, properly called crude oil, is a mixture of many different chemicals called hydrocarbons. These form the source of many different products, including gasoline, diesel fuel, lubricating oils, bottled gases, and compounds used for making various types of plastic.

KEY FACTS

● **Oil is an important raw material for industry.**

● **Large oil reserves remain in the rock layers under the world's rain forests.**

● **Searching for and producing oil is often damaging to the rain forest, especially along the roads and pipelines that service the oil wells and refineries.**

Oil is formed when plant remains become buried under layers of sand or mud, which turn into rock. Over millions of years underground, at great temperature and pressure, the plant remains are turned into crude oil. Thus oil is normally found far below the earth's surface, trapped between layers of rock, usually along with gas.

Looking for Oil

Oil exploration companies use several methods to try to find sources of oil, called reservoirs. If there is a likelihood of an oil reservoir in the rock layers, geologists use seismography to investigate further. They set off explosions to make shock waves that travel into the ground, listen for them to come back up, and figure out the depths of the layers of rock that reflected the waves. Carrying out seismic tests involves clearing only small areas of rain forest where helicopters can land with equipment. Companies must clear a much larger area, at least 1,600 feet (500 m) across, for an exploration well.

As the world's oil reserves are used up, oil companies are searching farther and wider for it. The areas where they are searching include under the world's rain forests. Companies have discovered extensive oil reserves in the Amazon River basin, New Guinea, the Philippines, and Indonesia.

It is not the recovery of oil itself that causes so much

Thousands of trees have been felled to make space for this oil exploration well in Kalimantan, Indonesia.

An oil pipeline in the Upper Amazon area of Ecuador. Clearing the forest has led to erosion gullies where the soil has been washed away.

damage to the rain forests but the construction of access roads and pipelines. They allow erosion to start and give settlers access to new areas of the forest. Accidental oil spills pollute rivers and kill wildlife.

The governments of these countries have sold the right to explore and drill for oil to international oil companies. Often local people have no say in the decision, nor are they employed by the companies. Most receive little benefit from the wealth that oil exploration brings.

Oil Companies Versus Local Peoples
In Colombia the U'wa people have been fighting to preserve their lands

from oil exploration, launching an international appeal to halt oil companies' work there. The U'wa homeland is one of the most endangered forests in the country, lying at the headwaters of the Orinoco River and covering sensitive cloud forest and rain forest systems. Just north of U'wa territory, an oil pipeline has spilled an estimated 1.7 million barrels of crude oil into nearby soil, rivers, and lakes. Guerrilla groups in the country view oil installations as strategic targets and bomb them frequently, causing massive pollution.

Some oil companies try to work with local people. In 1995 the Chevron oil company set up a community relations program, holding meetings with local people and environmental groups before beginning a seismic survey in Peru.

IN FOCUS

Yasuni National Park

Ecuador's Yasuni National Park was created in 1979, and ten years later UNESCO (United Nations Educational, Scientific, and Cultural Organization) declared it a Biosphere Heritage. However, since then the government has given permission to five companies to explore for oil in the park. The park is also home to the Huaorani people, who have tried to fight the continued exploitation of their lands. In January 1999 the Ecuadorian president issued a decree blocking future oil exploration in Yasuni. However, oil companies are continuing to pressure the government for permission to explore and extract oil, and their efforts look like they may succeed. A group of major oil companies is seeking to construct a new crude oil pipeline in Ecuador.

Check these out:
● Erosion ● Exploitation ● Exploration and Research ● Human Interference ● National Park ● Pollution

Okapi

The okapi (oe-KAH-pee) is one of the largest of the rain forest animals, but because it lives deep in central Africa's forests, it was unknown to biologists before 1901. Okapis live only in the northern parts of the Democratic Republic of the Congo, north of the Zaire River.

The okapi is the giraffe's nearest living relative. Because of its long neck and striped legs, it was once described as a cross between a giraffe and a zebra. Okapis are a deep reddish brown, with horizontal white stripes on the rump and front and back legs. Males have two short, skin-covered horns. Okapis grow to a height of about 8 feet (2.4 m). They browse on leaves and young shoots, which they rip from the trees with their long tongues, and occasionally eat fallen fruit.

Riverbanks and forest clearings are the main habitats of the okapis, for this is where the animals can find plenty of succulent young leaves. They feed by day and night. Their eyesight is quite poor, but excellent hearing enables them to sense danger. Leopards sometimes attack okapi calves, but the adults can defend themselves well by kicking out with their strong legs. Although the white stripes at the rear undoubtedly break up the animal's outline and make it

more difficult to see in the forest, this is probably not their main function. Each individual has a slightly different pattern, and this enables the calves to recognize and follow their own mothers.

Local people have hunted okapis for meat for thousands of years without harming the population, but other people are now invading the forests and hunting them. The okapi is becoming a rare animal. Although it is protected by law, it is impossible to stop the poaching in the vast African rain forest.

When immersed in rain forest vegetation, the okapi's white stripes and patches break up its outline very effectively and make it difficult to spot.

Check these out:
● Africa   ● Congo   ● Herbivore
● Poaching

The orangutan is the largest of the Asian apes. Its name means "man of the woods." Although only about 4 ½ feet (1.4 m) high when standing upright, a male orangutan can weigh as much as 200 pounds (90 kg). The males usually have beards, and their faces often resemble those of men. Young orangutans have orange-red hair that gets darker with age; older animals have deep brown hair.

Orangutans live only on the islands of Sumatra and Borneo, spending most of their time in the trees. They are not as fast or as agile as gibbons but swing slowly from branch to branch, holding on with their hook-shaped hands and feet, never letting go with one limb until they have a firm grip with another. Their arms are much longer than their legs. On the ground orangutans usually walk on all fours, although they can walk in an upright position, usually with their arms held above their heads.

Adult male orangutans develop broad cheek pads around their faces. The males with the biggest pads usually win any territorial battles because they scare the others away.

Orangutans have enormous appetites and often do nothing but eat. Fruits, including mangoes and durians, are their main foods, and the animals seem to know exactly when and where to go to find the trees with the best fruit. They also eat young leaves and insects and occasionally take nestling birds and eggs. Several individuals may gather in trees with plenty of fruit, but otherwise they usually live alone. Each individual has a home range covering several square miles. A female may have three or four babies during her lifetime; orangutans live for about 35 years.

Although the animals are not as rare as it was once thought, orangutan populations have fallen dramatically because the destruction of the rain forest has decreased their habitat. The remaining animals are strictly protected, with several healthy populations being maintained in national parks and other reserves.

Check these out:
- Ape
- Endangered Species
- Indonesia
- Primate

Glossary

Algae: plantlike organisms that live in colonies in water or wet places on land. They have no flowers and no true leaves or stems.

Anti-inflammatory: a substance that prevents inflammation in the body, which is characterized by pain, heat, and redness.

Aphid: a small sluggish insect with sucking mouthparts that commonly sucks the juices of plants.

Archaeology: the study of the remains of peoples from the past.

Binocular: the use of two eyes to focus on an object, which helps to determine the correct distance of the object from the viewer.

Biodiversity: a shortened term for biological diversity, which describes the variety of plants and animals in an area.

Biologist: a scientist who studies biology, the science of living things.

Bromeliad: any of over 1,000 plants of the pineapple family that have a crown of stiff, spiny leaves. Many bromeliads grow on trees.

Camouflage: a form of trickery or deception, particularly one involving the use of concealing colors and patterns, enabling an animal to avoid the attention of its enemies or its prey.

Canines: sharp teeth at the front corners of the mouth, used for piercing food or for killing prey.

Cannibalism: the act of catching and eating members of one's own species.

Canopy: the "roof" of the forest, composed of interlocking tree branches that cut off most of the light to the forest floor.

Clear-cutting: the cutting down of all of the trees in an area of forest.

Coniferous: trees with needle-shaped leaves and cones instead of flowers.

Drought: a period of very dry weather when rain fails to arrive.

Dry forest: forests with a long dry season and often only little rainfall.

Epiphyte: any plant that grows on another without taking any food from it.

Evolution: the process by which living organisms change from one form to another over a long period of time.

Germinate: when seeds take up water and begin to grow into a new plant.

Immunity: the ability of the body to resist disease and infection.

Inbreeding: mating between two animals that are closely related.

Incisors: the front teeth, usually flat or spade-shaped, used for cutting and nibbling.

Indigenous: people, animals, or plants that live naturally in an area.

Larva: a young insect that is markedly different from the adult and that has to pass through a pupal or chrysalis stage to reach maturity. Caterpillars, maggots, and young beetles are larvae.

Latex: a sticky liquid that oozes out of some plants when their stems are cut.

Leukemia: a disease in which the body produces far too many white blood cells.

Malaria: a human disease caused by a single-celled animal living in the red blood cells.

Maori: the people who are indigenous to New Zealand.

Mimicry: the copying of the shape, color, or behavior of one living organism by another.

Ore: a rock or mineral from which a metal can be extracted. For example, the mineral bauxite is the main ore of aluminum.

Photosynthesis: the process by which green plants combine water and carbon dioxide from the air to make simple sugars, which they use as energy-giving food.

Plantain: a large, starchy type of banana, commonly used for cooking.

Poaching: the hunting and killing of animals on other people's land or on protected land without permission.

Predatory: being an organism that catches and eats other organisms.

Primate: an animal belonging to the group of mammals that includes monkeys, apes, and humans.

Pupa: the stage in which the body of a larva is transformed into that of the adult. The pupa of a butterfly or a moth is often called a chrysalis.

Sacramental: of importance in religious ceremony.

Sexual reproduction: the production of the next generation of a living organism by means of mating between male and female animals or by pollination in plants.

Shoal: a sandbank or shallow water.

Slash and burn: a method of farming employed in rain forest areas. The farmers cut down and burn the forest to make room to plant crops.

Spore: a minute, dustlike reproductive cell released by mosses, liverworts, ferns, and fungi.

Subtropical: inhabiting the regions between the Tropics and the temperate areas.

Temperate: regions that lie between the subtropics and polar regions and that experience warm summers and cold winters.

Tropics: the regions on either side of the equator that remain warm throughout the year.

Watershed: an area drained by a river.

Index

All numbers in *italics* indicate photographs.

Amazon River basin 376, 378, 380–381, 416
ants 415
    weaver 405
anteaters 407
antelope, nilgai 390
armadillos 407
aye-ayes 408

bacteria 415
bats 363, 407, 409
bear, black 397, 413
beaver 399
bees 403
biodiversity 395, 400
birds 389, 397, 400, 403–404, 410, 412
    Asian fairy bluebird 397
    boobies 363
    bowerbirds 399
    cormorants 363
    ducks 412
    eagles 403, 412
        crowned 403
    egrets 363
    frigates 363
    geese 412
    hawks 403
    herons 412
    hummingbirds 376, 404

    kingfishers 412
    kiwis 406
    macaws 400
    nightjars 410
    oropendolas 403, 405
        chestnut-headed *404*
    ovenbirds 405
    owls 407–410, 412
        sooty *409*
    parrots 400
        crimson rosella 399
    rainbow pitta 405
    scarlet ibis 363
    scarlet minivet 397
    sunbirds 376
    swifts 405
        Asian palm 405
    tailorbirds 404
    tyrant flycatchers 376
    warblers 376
    wood ibises 376
    woodpeckers 389, 412
    wood storks 376
    yellow-green vireos 376
Borneo 376
Brazil 367, 380–381
bromeliads 391
bug, peanut *401*, 402

camouflage 364–365, 402
carnivorous plants 415
Caroni swamp, Trinidad 363
cats 409–410

cattle ranching 380
chimpanzees 399, 405
Chiricoa people 376
clear-cutting 411
cockroaches 407, 409
Colombia 417
Congo River 370
Costa Rica 400
cougar, or mountain lion 412–413
crickets 408
    wetas 406
crocodiles and caimans 405, 408
curare 375

Darwin, Charles 402, *402*
decomposers 415
deer 363, 407–408
    black-tailed 413
    chital 363
    sambar 390
    spotted 390
deforestation 363, *363*, 380
diseases 372–375, 379, 381, 391

elephants 390, 397
elk 399, 413
    Roosevelt elk *413*
epiphytes 393
erosion 380
evolution 402

ferns 412
fish 363, 376, 408
    paradise 403
    salmon 412
flooding 376
foxes 409
frog 408
    red-eyed leaf 399
fungi 415

galagos 408
gaur 390
gorillas 405
    mountain *405*
    western lowland 399
Grand Carajas Program 381
Guahibo people 376

Huaorani people 417
hydroelectric dams 380–381

India 389
Indonesia 416
invertebrates 410

jaguars 408

leeches 389
lemurs 396
leopards 363, 390, 408
leukemia 375
lichens 412
logging 379–380
lorises 408
    slow loris *408*

malaria 373, 391
mammals 410
mangrove forest 362–363, *362*, 394
mantises 364–365, *364–365*
    Archimantis 364
marmosets and tamarins 366–367, 387
    common marmosets 366
    emperor tamarin 367, *367*
    golden lion tamarin 367
    pygmy marmoset *366*
    saddle-back tamarin 367
Maya people 368–369, *368–369*
Mbuti people 370–371, *370–371*
medicinal plants 372–375
mice 408
migration 376
millipedes 377, *377*
Mineracao Rio do Norte 381
mining 378–381, *378–381*
mink 412
Miskito people 382–383, *382–383*
mongooses 384, 409
    crab-eating 384
    ring-tailed 384, *384*
    stripe-necked 384
monkeys 385–388
    capuchins 385
    colobus 385–386, *388*
    DeBrazza's 385
    douroucouli, or night monkey 388, *407*, 408
    guenons 386–387
    howler 386–387

langurs 386
    douc *385*
    leaf 386
    macaque 386
        bonnet 390
        pig-tailed 385
        stump-tailed 390
    mandrills 386–387, *387*
    mangabeys 386–387
    proboscis 386, *386*
    rhesus 388
    spider 385
    squirrel 387
    titi 387
    uakaris 387
monsoon rain forest 389–390, *389*
mosquitoes 381, 391, *391*
mosses 390, 392–393, *392-393*, 412
    liverworts 393
moths 410
mudskippers 363, 394, *394*

national parks 389–390, 395–400
    Bwindi National Park *399*
    Chitwan National Park 395, 397
    Cross River National Park 399
    Guatopo National Park 397
    Kerinci National Park 397
    Khao Yai National Park *395*, 397
    Korup National Park 395, 398–399
    Kuna Indian Forest Park 396
    La Amistad 400
    Lamington National Park 399
    Manú National Park 399–400, *400*
    Olympic National Park *392*, 399, 413
    Periyar National Park 389, *389*, 397
    Ranomafana 396, *396*
    Taman Negara National Park 397, *397*
    Westland National Park *406*
    Yasuni National Park 417
natural selection 401–402
nest and nest-building 403–405, *403–405*
New Guinea 416
New Zealand 406, *406*
nitrogen cycle *414*
nocturnal animals 407–410
North America 411–413, *41.*
nurse logs 412
nutrients 362-363, 414–415
nutrient cycle 414–415

oil exploration 416–417
okapis 418, *418*
orangutans 405, 419, *419*
orchids 390
Orinoco River 376, 417
otters 399, 412

Panama Canal 391
Peru 417, 399–400
Philippines 416
pigs, bearded 376, *376*
plantations 373
poaching 418
pollution 379, 381, 417
possums 399, 408

prawns 363
primates 398, 400, 405
quetzals 400
quolls, spotted tail 408

rainfall 389–390, 406, 411
roots 362-363
rosy periwinkle 375, *375*

seasons 376, 389-390
shrews 410
shrimp 363
slash and burn agriculture 368, 380
snails 410
snakes 407–408
spiders 408–409
    net-casting *410*
squirrels 390, 403, 412
    flying 399
        northern 412, *412*
    Malabar 397
symbiosis 415

tapirs 398
temperate rain forest 411–413
termites 403–404
tigers 363, 390, 397, 408–409
tourism 396–400
trees 389
    beeches 406
    birch 390
    casaurina 390
    chestnut 390
    cinchona 373
    cinnamon 390
    conifers 412–413
    Douglas fir 412
    flame-of-the-forest 390, *390*
    gewa 362
    goran 362
    Indian rosewood 390
    mahoganies 390
    magnolia 390
    mountain ebony 390
    nipa palms 362
    nutmeg 390
    pines 390
        matai, or black pine 406
        rimu, or red pine 406
    plum 390
    rata 406
    sandalwood 390
    Sitka spruce 412
    Sonneratia 362
    sundri 362
    teak 389
    western hemlock 412
    western red cedar 412

U'wa people 417

voles, red-backed 412

wasps *403*, 405
    paper 403
    potter 403
watershed 397

yellow fever 391